USING & PROGRAMMING THE
ZX81/TS1000
INCLUDING READY-TO-RUN PROGRAMS

USING & PROGRAMMING THE
ZX81/TS1000
INCLUDING READY-TO-RUN PROGRAMS
BY ALBERT N. SICKLER

TAB BOOKS Inc.
BLUE RIDGE SUMMIT, PA. 17214

FIRST EDITION

FIRST PRINTING

Printed in the United States of America

Library of Congress Cataloging in Publication Data

Sickler, Albert N.
Using and programming the ZX81/TS1000, including ready-to-run programs.

Includes index.
1. Sinclair ZX81 (Computer)—Programming. 2. Timex 1000 (Computer)—Programming. 3. Basic (Computer program language) I. Title.
QA76.8.S625S5 1983 001.64 83-4938
ISBN 0-8306-0117-1
ISBN 0-8306-0617-3 (pbk.)

Cover photograph courtesy of the Ziegler Photography Studio of Waynesboro, PA.

Contents

How to Use This Book

NOT LIKE THIS!

Most new owners of the ZX81 have very little experience in microcomputer use; in many cases they will have bought the ZX81 in order to gain experience in this fascinating field. The ZX81 is an ideal computer for this purpose as it is inexpensive, simple to operate, and enables the owner to design and run his own programs.

With this in mind we have written a book to help the beginner learn about his new computer. The first section includes an introduction to the essential concepts of hardware and software and highlights ZX81 characteristics, showing how it can be used and expanded. This is followed by a completed course in BASIC programming, tailored to the specific capabilities of the ZX81. Generally speaking the ZX81 BASIC programming language is the same as the standard BASIC language, but there are a few minor differences and a number of interesting additions. The book also includes numerous examples. These have been kept very simple, so that the effect of different operations can be seen as clearly as possible. Many of the examples have been designed to illustrate to the beginner what constitutes a good program. Towards the end of the book you will find practical information on such topics as the graphic symbols used and the codes used for error messages.

You will probably find it helpful to browse through the book first and begin to familiarize yourself with the various subjects covered. It is best if you then begin by reading the first six chapters instead of starting to press keys at random. Pressing keys at random will not damage the ZX81, of course, but just pressing keys to see what happens could easily make you feel that the ZX81 is too complicated to understand, which is not true at all. If you first have a basic grasp of the main principles, you will not be daunted by the large number of characters on the keyboard. Instead, you will be encouraged by the fact that you already understand what many of them are for and how to use them.

We hope that you will enjoy using the ZX81. Programming can be a useful as well as an entertaining activity.

This book can also be used with the ZX80, but only if the latter is provided with the upgraded version of BASIC.

Chapter 1
Hardware and Software

The verb *to compute* means *to calculate*. This might give you the impression that a computer is a sort of calculator. To merely call it a calculator does not do it justice, as a computer is capable of much more than just carrying out calculations. The real work of a computer is processing information according to a given set of instructions. The information to be processed may consist of numbers; of patterns (certain shapes that can be displayed on a TV screen, for example), of letters (just think of all the possible applications in word processing), of musical notes, and so on.

When we use the term *instructions*, we are not only thinking of arithmetic operations such as addition, subtraction, multiplication, and division, but also of commands such as "clear the screen".

Two common terms used in the computer world are *hardware* and *software*, and we shall deal with these concepts in some detail further on. Basically, hardware refers to the actual physical units of a computer system (components, keyboard, and so on), whereas software is the term used for the instructions we can give the computer, that is the programs.

HARDWARE

A computer, or data processor, can be diagrammatically represented as in Fig. 1-1.

The term hardware, therefore, refers to all of the physical parts of the computer system, such as the electronic components, keyboard, and visual display units. The central processing unit (CPU) and the memory are also part of the hardware of the computer.

The central processing unit is the real heart of the computer. This unit actually carries out the instructions given to it. The sets of instructions are stored in the memory. When it has a task to perform, the computer reads these instructions one by one from the memory and carries them out. Since a memory can only contain series of ones and zeros, the instructions must be coded in these digits. The user therefore needs to master a simple language in which to give instructions, and this simple language is known as BASIC.

Every keystroke (on the keyboard) is automatically converted electronically into a series of ones and zeros. In the same way, as terms from our programming language are keyed into the computer, they are converted into sets of ones and zeros. These one-and-zero instructions will then produce the required result. The ZX81 uses a very well-known type of CPU, known as the Z80(A), to achieve this. All this information is particularly important when programming with instructions that do not need to be interpreted first, but can be obeyed directly by the central processing unit. These are called machine codes or machine instructions. For a beginner this would be rather indigestible material, so it is important to learn BASIC first. The BASIC language will in most cases be adequate for all of your problems.

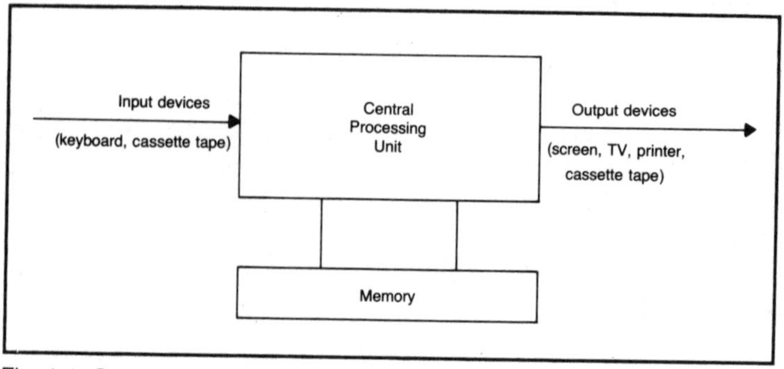

Fig. 1-1. General representation of a computer.

As you can see in Fig. 1-1, the two main types of *input device* are the keyboard and the cassette tape. These are two methods of supplying the computer with information. *Information* is the data that needs to be processed; it is also the series of instructions that indicate what exactly needs to be done. Such a series of instructions is called a *program*, and the preparation of such a set of instructions is referred to as *programming*. By pressing various keys on the keyboard, we can "input" the necessary program.

The ZX81 keyboard differs considerably from the standard typewriter keyboard, the keyboard with which we are all most familiar. The most obvious difference is the large number of characters and symbols found on the ZX81. Although these may at first appear daunting, we will discuss the keyboard in great detail later on, and you will find that it is quite straightforward.

The use of a cassette recorder as an input device is less obvious and will be discussed more fully in Chapter 19. At this stage it is only essential for you to understand that cassettes are used mainly to store and run individual programs. Sinclair has in fact produced a number of ready-made programs.

Output devices are methods by which information can be displayed or recorded on a TV screen, a printer, or on a cassette tape for example.

The beginner only needs a screen. The results of all kinds of calculations as well as animated graphics (which can be used in various games) can be displayed on the screen. The ZX81 uses an ordinary TV screen (black and white or color). It can operate in two ways: at a relatively slow speed, called slow mode, and at a relatively fast speed, called fast mode. In slow mode the screen is continuously illuminated, whereas in fast mode the screen darkens while the calculations are being carried out. This is because the computer carries out the calculations at such high speed that there is no time to show intermediate results.

The ZX81 is designed in such a way that the TV screen is subdivided into 24 horizontal rows, usually referred to as lines, with 32 columns per horizontal line. The bottom two lines are permanently reserved for the display of coding information. The top 22 horizontal lines (each subdivided into 32 sections) are entirely available for the user to fill with characters (letters, numbers, and graphic symbols).

Information can also be stored on cassette tape or can be printed on a printer. The main advantage of a printer is that it provides hard copy, which can be kept as a permanent record, enabling the programmer to check the results of a certain program at any time to see whether everything has gone according to plan. Sinclair has designed a special printer for the ZX81 and it is the only printer that can be linked to this computer.

The central processing unit constantly exchanges information with the memory. This means that combinations of ones and zeros are retrieved (or read) from the memory and combinations of ones and zeros are stored (or written) in the memory. For the computer to be able to function properly, therefore, part of the memory must be able to read and write sets of ones and zeros (data) at random places in the memory. This facility is referred to as RAM (random access memory). The standard ZX81 contains a RAM that can be compared with a filing cabinet with 1024 files. Each file contains eight compartments in which the numbers one or zero can be stored. These files are normally referred to as *characters*.

In computer jargon this is known as 1K (or 1024) characters (or files) of 8 bits (or ones and/or zeros). An 8-bit unit is sometimes referred to as a *byte*. The standard RAM is sufficient for the beginner experimenting with different instructions, but is not a very large unit. The serious user will need the 16K RAM Pack, a separate memory expansion pack produced by Sinclair. The programs that fit in the standard memory generally consist of no more than a few dozens lines (although this does depend on the nature of the program, for example, whether it contains a large number of variables, whether a large amount of text needs to be displayed on the screen and so on).

The example programs in this book can all be carried out with the standard available memory.

In addition to the RAM, the ZX81 also contains a ROM (read only memory). The special characteristic of this type of memory is that it cannot be used to store data; the user can only read information from it. In the ROM the manufacturer has stored ready-made programs, including the program that translates the BASIC instructions typed in by you into the machine codes which will produce the required result. This program, contained in the ROM, is called the *BASIC interpreter*.

SOFTWARE

The programs stored in the ROM, the BASIC interpreter, and the machine codes are all part of the software. *Software* is a general term for programs and everything connected with them. It has been said that the software determines the real power of a computer. In a sense this is absolutely true because only a good program will use the computer's capabilities to the maximum. The ZX81 is a particularly attractive machine because it can be used to run "powerful" BASIC programs straightaway.

There are three main categories of software. Theses are:

1. Programs that control the operation of the computer itself. These are the programs already stored in the ROM by the manufacturer.
2. Programs that can be written by the user.
3. Programs that can be bought ready-made and can be run immediately.

The programs that control the operation of the machine itself are sometimes referred to as the *operating system*. In the case of smaller machines such as the ZX81 the name *monitor* is sometimes used.

Programs written by the user are very important as many users have bought this computer to gain programming experience. The language most commonly used to program the ZX81 is BASIC.

Ready-made programs are also important as an increasing number of programs are supplied on cassette tape, ready for use. Don't forget that only cassettes stating explicity that they are suitable for the ZX81 can be used.

It is advisable to store all usable programs on cassette from the start, complete with proper documentation, so that you can locate and re-use the program you want without difficulty.

Chapter 2
Connecting and Switching on the Computer

Before you can use the ZX81, you must, of course, connect it properly. The procedure is as follows.

1. Connect the ZX81 to a television (black and white or color), using the lead provided. One end of the lead fits in the antenna socket of the television and the other end fits into the connector marked "TV" on the ZX81.
2. Connect the lead from the power supply unit to the ZX81 by plugging the jack plug into the connector marked "9 Vdc in."
3. Switch on the television and tune to channel 3 (VHF).
4. Plug the power supply into the mains.
5. Tune the television until it gives the picture in Fig. 2-1.

In Chapter 19 you will find instructions for connecting the cassette recorder and the printer.

If you have a RAM module (memory expansion pack), all you need to do is disconnect the mains supply, then slide the module into the groove provided. This can only be done in one way and should not give you any problems.

Fig. 2-1. The screen after the ZX81 is installed and turned on.

When the computer is disconnected by pulling out the 9 Vdc in plug, all information is lost, including the program you have just designed. It is therefore essential that you use a cassette recorder when you write your own programs so that you can save them for future use.

Sometimes the fact that everything will be "clean" when the computer is switched on again can be an advantage. When you are completely stuck and the machine seems to react very strangely to your commands, the best thing to do is to disconnect the machine and then plug it in again. By doing this you can start again with a clean slate, but the ZX81 will react properly.

Chapter 3

A First BASIC Program

Now that the ZX81 is set up and connected, it is tempting to start trying to use the keyboard, but it is important to have some knowledge of BASIC before you start typing. If you do not, it will be impossible for you to understand the keyboard properly, and you may well be put off by the large number of symbols. In this chapter, therefore, we will deal with the basic facts, and it is important to read these carefully. In the next chapter you will be told how to use the keyboard and will be able to start entering a program.

> WARNING:
> Do not start typing until you have read this chapter. In the next chapter you will be told how to use the keyboard.

Many people still associate the word "programming" with an elite few expert mathematicians. In this chapter you will see that programming is not difficult, and that anyone can enjoy it.

A program is a series of instructions. When the computer carries out the successive instructions the desired result appears on the screen. In BASIC programming each instruction is written on a separate line. Each line must be preceded by a line number, which must always be a positive number. The lines must be numbered in ascending order; but they do not have to run consecutively. For example, 1, 2, 3, 4, 5 is a perfectly correct sequence of line numbers, but it does not offer any opportunity for additional instructions to be inserted at a later stage. If, however, the lines are numbered 10, 20, 30, 40, and 50, it will be possible for you to insert nine additional lines between every two successive lines. Our example programs will therefore always be numbered in ascending increments of ten.

The line numbers will prove to be very useful for two reasons.

1. Line numbers are useful when writing or altering a program.
2. Later you will learn how to include jump instructions in a program. With these jump instructions the line numbers act as labels (or reference addresses) to which the program is to jump.

The program below calculates the interest return on a capital of $1100 over one year when the interest rate is 8 percent. The interest return can be found by multiplying the capital by 0.08. The result (the calculated interest return) is to be printed on the screen.

This is the complete program.

```
1Ø  LET CAP=11ØØ
20  LET INTEREST=ØØ8
3Ø  LET AMOUNT=CAP*INTEREST
4Ø  PRINT AMOUNT
```

As a result of this program, the number 88 should appear on the screen. Every line of the program starts with a line number in the sequence 10, 20, 30, 40, as discussed.

You will notice that the multiplication sign is represented by the symbol * rather than by a times sign (×) to prevent possible confusion with the letter X. For the same reason the number 0 is written Ø to prevent confusion with the capital letter O.

> ALWAYS REMEMBER:
> On the keyboard the digit 0 is represented by Ø. The multiplication sign is represented by *.

In ordinary English, the first line of the program would read:
10 let CAP be equal to 1100.

In other words, the capital is $1100. On "reading" this instruction the computer reserves a memory space, which it labels CAP. This memory space can be pictured as a box in which the computer can store a number. According to the first instruction of our BASIC program the value 1100 is to be stored in the box labeled CAP. CAP could of course be used to store a different value, and this capacity to store a variable quantity is the reason why a "box" or memory space is called a *variable*. A variable is, therefore, simply a labeled box, or memory space, in which a number can be stored.

Each variable has its own name, or label, in BASIC. With the ZX81, the choice of name is very flexible. The only restrictions are that the name must always consist of letters, spaces, and digits and the first character must always be a letter.

Here are a few examples of correct names:

INTEREST
INTEREST AMOUNT
X
UNKNOWN 1
ZX81

The following examples show incorrect names:

4 TIMES
WELL?

The first example is incorrect because it starts with a number. The second is incorrect because it uses a question mark.

The ZX81 therefore allows a great deal more freedom than the standard version of BASIC used with other computers, and this gives the programmer the ability to use imaginative and appropriate names.

When selecting names for a program, it is important to choose names that give the person reading the program a clear idea of the purpose and content of the program. For example, the following program will give the same result as the original program example.

```
 1  LET A=11ØØ
23  LET B3=Ø.Ø8
47  LET C7B=A*B3
48  PRINT C7B
```

For this program, however, the names are completely arbitrary. Anyone reading the program for the first time would have no indication of what the program was intended to do. In addition, the odd sequence of line numbers is unnecessarily confusing.

It is also a good idea to select fairly short names. This is because the standard ZX81 does not have a very large memory. Since each letter of a name occupies a byte (consisting of eight bits), a program with a large number of variables will quickly use up the available memory. This is why the name CAP is a better choice than the more obvious name CAPITAL. Owners of a ZX81 with the memory expansion pack should choose names according to the directions provided with the pack.

Looking at the program example again, you see that the second line is:

```
20  LET INTEREST=0.08
```

This states that the value of 0.08 is to be assigned to the variable named INTEREST.

The third line is:

```
30  LET AMOUNT=CAP*INTEREST
```

This line says that the value assigned to the variable named AMOUNT will be the number obtained by multiplying CAP by INTEREST.AMOUNT will therefore have the value 1100 × 0.08 = 88.

The last line of the program is:

```
40  PRINT AMOUNT
```

This contains a PRINT instruction which indicates that the value of AMOUNT is to be printed on the screen.

With most versions of BASIC, a program must finish with an END instruction. For example:

```
50  END
```

ZX81 BASIC allows you to omit the final END instruction (in fact it is impossible to add this instruction).

In the next chapter, you will be able to key this program into the computer, but for the moment it is sufficient to understand that the example program is a complete (correct) program which can be stored in the computer's memory to be executed when a certain command is given. As a result of the necessary command the computer will carry out the instructions one by one. Thus the first instruction will cause the computer to create a storage space labeled CAP. In this space the number 1100 is stored, using the binary notation (in which numbers are represented by ones and zeros). Next, the space labeled INTEREST is reserved, in which the number 0.08 is stored. Then the space named AMOUNT is reserved, the value 1100 × 0.08 is calculated, and the result is stored in AMOUNT.

Finally the contents of the storage space labeled AMOUNT are displayed on the screen by using the PRINT instruction. It is not printed as a series of ones and zeros (which is the binary notation in which the amount has been stored in the memory) but in decimal numbers which are easy to recognize and understand.

The program uses digits (to represent line numbers and numbers), words (such as LET and PRINT, which in BASIC have a special meaning), and names spelled by means of letters and digits. These are facts you need to be familiar with in order to understand the next chapter, which explains how the program is typed into the computer.

Chapter 4
How to Execute the First BASIC Program

Now that you know the basic facts, you can program the ZX81 to carry out the example interest calculation.

First, connect and switch on the computer following the instructions in Chapter 2. In the bottom left-hand corner of the screen, the letter K will appear in *inverse video*, that is a white K in a black square. This is known as a *cursor*. The complete program is:

```
10  LET CAP=1100
20  LET INTEREST=0.08
30  LET AMOUNT=CAP*INTEREST
40  PRINT AMOUNT
```

It is obvious that the first thing you must do is to type in the program, but before actually touching the keyboard, you must understand how it works.

THE KEYBOARD

The ZX81 has a touch-sensitive keyboard, so the keys just need to be pressed lightly.

Figure 4-1 shows the complete keyboard. Each key shows one main symbol and up to four other symbols, some of which are graphic symbols: squares which have been filled in in certain ways. These graphic symbols can be typed only if certain other keys are pressed first. It is not necessary to understand these symbols for our first program. They are, however, explained in Chapter 18.

Above the graphic symbols are some red symbols. For example, above the key with the main symbol A, STOP is marked in red. Many of these so-called symbols are in fact complete words, but for clarity and simplicity all the words and terms on the keyboard will be referred to as symbols. The symbols marked in red can be typed by simultaneously holding down the SHIFT key (which is also marked in red). This corresponds exactly to the operation of the shift key on an ordinary typewriter.

> REMEMBER:
> The SHIFT key must be held down while typing a red symbol.

Do not experiment with this now, as you might be faced with some strange situations.

There are also symbols above and below the keys. The symbols above the keys consist mainly of the keywords used in BASIC. These special instructions are frequently used in programming and evoke a particular response from the computer. In any BASIC program, each line number must be followed by a keyword. In our example program, the keywords LET and PRINT were used. When the computer expects such a keyword, this is indicated by the letter K in the bottom left-hand corner of the screen. The letter K stands for keyword, a *reserved word*. When the K appears, you know that

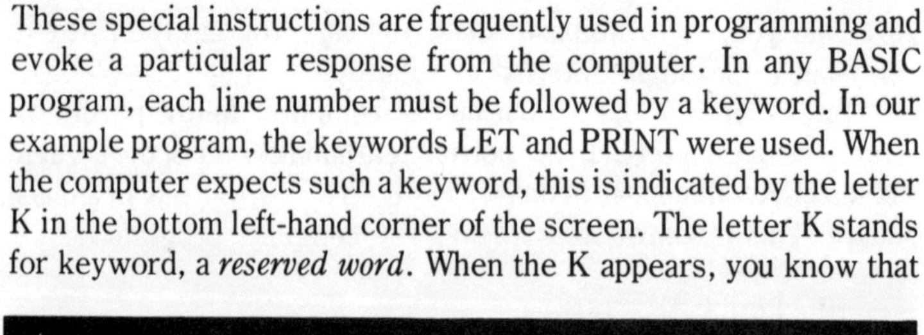

Fig. 4-1. The ZX81 keyboard.

the computer is expecting a keyword, such as LET or PRINT, so you just need to press the appropriate key and the keyword will automatically come up on the screen. For example, if the computer is expecting a keyword, indicated by the letter K appearing in the bottom left-hand corner, and you press the L key, the complete word LET will appear on the screen.

Finally there are symbols and terms underneath the keys on the keyboard. These symbols represent pre-programmed functions. In order to type such functions (which will be explained in following chapters), first type FUNCTION (by pressing SHIFT and NEW LINE). When FUNCTION has been typed, the cursor will change to the letter F, indicating that the computer is now expecting the name of a function. If you now press a key with a symbol written under it on the keyboard, the latter symbol will appear on the screen.

TYPING THE PROGRAM

Having looked at the keyboard, you can now start to use it by typing the example program.

First press keys 1 and 0 which form the first line number of the program. Next we need to type LET. To do this, press the key under the word LET (the L key). The word LET will now be displayed on the screen with a space between 10 and LET. The computer displays LET rather than L because the line number 10 will automatically be followed by a keyword and the letter L is not a keyword.

The cursor in the bottom left-hand corner will now change to L, indicating that the computer now expects you to type a letter.

Now type:

```
CAP=
```

The symbol = can be typed by depressing SHIFT while you type L, as the = symbol is found on the L key. Then type:

```
11ØØ
```

Remember that the number 0 is represented by Ø.

If that line is correct, press NEW LINE. The line which has just been typed will appear at the top of the screen, together with a second cursor, an arrow >, following the 10. You can ignore the arrow cursor for the moment, as it will be explained in more detail in Chapter 6.

If you have already made a mistake and the line is not correct, the best thing to do is to switch off the machine and then switch it on again and repeat the preceding procedure. If you have simply made a wrong keystroke, this can be deleted immediately by depressing the SHIFT key while you type RUBOUT. You can also delete a whole line in this way by holding down the SHIFT key and pressing the RUBOUT key repeatedly. More elegant methods of correcting errors will be described in Chapter 6.

Once the first line is typed correctly, you can continue. As a result of typing NEW LINE, the cursor will have changed back to K to indicate that a line number or keyword is expected. Now type:

```
2Ø   LET
```

LET will appear automatically when you press the L key as the computer expects a keyword after the line number. Then type:

```
INTEREST=Ø.Ø8
NEW LINE
```

As a result of pressing NEW LINE, the line which has just been typed will be placed under the first line.

Continue to type the next two lines in the same way. Don't forget that PRINT is another keyword, so after 40 you simply type

```
1Ø  LET CAP=11ØØ
2Ø  LET INTEREST=Ø.Ø8
3Ø  LET AMOUNT=CAP*INTEREST
4Ø>PRINT AMOUNT







K
```

Fig. 4-2. The screen display after the first four program lines have been typed.

P. Also remember that keywords such as LET and PRINT are automatically preceded and followed by a space. Whenever you are not dealing with keywords, you should type spaces separately by pressing the SPACE key at the bottom right-hand corner of the keyboard. If you have done all this correctly, the screen will look like Fig. 4-2.

RUNNING THE PROGRAM

Now you can run the program. To make the ZX81 execute the program, first give a command. Commands are special keywords that are activated by pressing a single key (provided, as before, that the K cursor is displayed on the screen). They differ from instructions in some respects. First, it is not necessary to type a line number, since a command is not an instruction that forms part of a complete program. Second, a command must be obeyed directly by the computer. The most common commands are NEW, LIST, and RUN.

When the NEW command is given, the entire memory is cleared. This command is used when you start to type a new program. When this command is given, the previous program is lost.

The LIST command causes the computer is display the program on the screen. A program display is sometimes called a *listing*. If a program contains more lines than can be displayed on the screen, parts of the program can be displayed by entering LIST followed by a line number. The screen will then display the program from that line onward.

The command RUN makes the computer carry out the program. After RUN, you can enter a line number to indicate that you want to run the program starting with that particular line. Each command must be completed by pressing NEW LINE.

To run the example program, press RUN, NEW LINE. The answer 88 will appear in the top left-hand corner. In the bottom left-hand corner you will see:

```
Ø/4Ø
```

The 0 indicates that no errors were found during the running of the program. The number 40 confirms the number of the last line of the program. If NEW LINE is pressed again, the program listing will reappear. The program can be run as often as necessary. Each time RUN is typed, the answer will appear again.

The LIST and NEW commands are simple to operate. First give the command:

```
LIST 3Ø
```

A program listing will appear, starting with line 30. To check that the first part of the program has not been lost, type:

```
LIST
```

and the complete program will reappear. It is also possible to run the program again by giving the RUN command.

Typing the NEW command causes the memory to be cleared, so it is important to take care when using this command.

Type:

```
NEW
```

If you now give the LIST command the screen shows only the message 0/0 and the program listing has dissappeared. The memory has been cleared, and the last program can no longer be executed.

Chapter 5
General Procedures for Writing a Program

This chapter examines how to write a good program. The program designed in Chapter 4 was very simple. The interest calculation it carried out could in fact easily be done on paper rather than on a computer. But this example program can be expanded so that more complicated calculations can be carried out. It is totally immaterial to the computer whether the program is complicated or not!

When a computer is needed to solve a problem, the user must write a program, which involves a series of steps.

1. Define the problem.
2. Find a method of solving the problem.
3. Design a program on the basis of the method found.
4. Test the program.
5. Document the program.

The simplest way to illustrate these different stages is with a simple example.

Imagine that you want to find the sum of a series of numbers or terms. The series consists of the numbers 1, 2, 3, 4 and so on up to and including 100. In other words, the first number is 1 and each subsequent number is found by adding 1 to the last number. The final number of the series is 100. This completes the first step, defining the problem.

The second step is to find a method to solve the problem. The method of solving a particular problem is sometimes called the *algorithm*. An algorithm is a series of procedural steps that lead to the required solution of a problem. If no method can be found, then this is where the programming ends. But with our example problem, the solution is quite obvious: add 1 and 2, then add 3 to the total, then add 4, and so on. A program performing these operations might look like this:

```
  10  LET TERM 1=1
  20  LET TERM 2=2
  30  LET TERM 3=3
  . . . . . . . . . . . .
         etc.
1000  LET TERM 100=100
1010  LET SUM=(TERM1+TERM2+...etc. +TERM100)
1020  PRINT SUM
```

This is a rather complicated and rigid method, however. If you were ever faced with a similar problem—for example, having to determine the sum of a series of numbers where each number is found by adding a constant to each previous number—this solution would be totally inadequate.

It is therefore necessary to consider the problem more closely. By doing this, you will see that when you add terms 1 and 100, 2 and 99, 3 and 98, the result is always 101. Thus the series can be divided into 50 pairs of terms, each of which adds up to 101. Consequently the total sum can be found by multiplying the number of pairs by the sum of the first and last terms:

NUMBER OF PAIRS * (FIRST+LAST)

The number of pairs is equal to the number of terms divided by 2. A total number is often represented by the letter N, therefore this can be represented by:

$$\frac{N}{2} * (FIRST+LAST)$$

This completes the second step. The formula provides a good method of solving the problem, and it can easily be translated into a BASIC program.

Step 3 consists of converting the method into a BASIC program. If the method seems rather complicated, try to separate it into a number of more or less independent sections. On a separate list write down the meaning of the variables and the name given to each variable in the program. Then start to convert the method into a series of instructions. The complete list of instructions will be the final BASIC program. In this case the method is simple and it will therefore be sufficient to give the program:

```
10  LET FIRST=1
20  LET LAST=100
30  LET N=100
40  LET SUM=N/2*(FIRST+LAST)
50  PRINT SUM
```

The answer should be 5050.

The parentheses in expressions such as (FIRST+LAST) are used in the same way as in "ordinary" algebra. The entire formula for the sum must be typed on one line. The 2 is placed beside the / and not below the N. The latter position might cause problems when it comes to deciding whether the multiplication 2*(FIRST+LAST) should be carried out first (which would of course be incorrect) or whether the division N/2 must come first, after which the result of the division is multiplied by the expression in brackets (which would be the correct method). Any doubts could be dispelled by the use of extra parentheses:

```
40  LET SUM=(N/2)*(FIRST+LAST)
```

In this case, however, this is not necessary as multiplication and division have *equal priority*, that is neither needs to be given priority and the calculation can simply be carried out from left to right. This rule differs clearly from the one most people were taught in school, where multiplication always has priority over division. In BASIC, addition and subtraction also have equal priority and are performed from left to right in an expression. In BASIC, multiplication and division do have priority over addition and subtraction. In Appendix D you will find detailed instructions concerning the method of working out expressions. You will encounter few problems, however, if you stick to the rule: if in doubt, use parentheses.

Step 4, testing the program, can create serious problems. The first thing to do is to run the programs. If no unexpected error report appears while the program is running, you can take this as a first indication that all is well. It is, however, no guarantee that the program is correct. What is more, you can never be completely sure that a program is completely free of errors. If instead of:

```
10 LET FIRST=1
```

you had typed:

```
20 LET FIRST=2
```

the computer would not report that anything was wrong. If you did not discover the mistake yourself in good time, you might simply assume that you would receive the correct answer when running the program. In this particular case, the answer could easily be checked by working out the calculation on paper, and the error would be discovered when the two answers were compared. But once you have mastered the ZX81, you will be dealing with programs which it would be virtually impossible to work out without the computer.

When testing a program it is therefore necessary to apply the following strategies.

1. Find out whether any solutions to the problem have been found by other methods and compare the answers with the results of your own program.
2. Try to perform a similar calculation using simple numbers.
3. In the case of a program that is to be used frequently as part of a regular routine; be particularly careful and work out individual sections of the program on paper wherever possible.
4. Include extra PRINT instructions to print intermediate results. By studying the intermediate results, you can follow and check the program step by step.

In this case you can test the procedure by using a series that shows the same characteristics but that is considerably less complicated. Consider for instance the series: 1, 2, 3, and 4 to which the formula we found would of course be equally applicable, and could be tested. The test program would then be:

```
10  LET FIRST=1
20  LET LAST=4
30  LET N=4
40  LET SUM=N/2*(FIRST+LAST)
50  PRINT SUM
```

The final step, step 5, is usually skipped out of sheer laziness, which often brings its own punishment. If this simple calculation is correct using your program, then the more complicated calculation should also be correct.

The documentation should always include the following items.

1. A short description of the problem.
2. A short description of the method of solving it.
3. A listing of the program.
4. Directions for the input of data.
5. An example of the text that will appear when the program is run.

Chapter 6
Error Correction

This chapter deals with the correction of errors. The ZX81 provides a number of handy facilities for error correction and also for expanding a program. The ZX81 also checks, while each line is being typed, whether that line includes any obvious mistakes. If there is an obvious error, the S (for syntax) cursor appears just to the left of the error. Once an S cursor appears, it will be impossible to add that line to the rest of the program, however hard you press the NEW LINE key.

Start with the following familiar program:

```
10 LET FIRST=1
20 LET LAST=100
30 LET N=100
40 LET SUM=N/2*(FIRST+LAST)
50 PRINT SUM
```

Enter this program as described in Chapter 5. First type NEW before typing in the program in order to clear the memory. When the program has been typed in, the program cursor will be pointing to line 50.

Suppose that as well as the value of SUM, you also wish to print out the values of FIRST, LAST, and N for checking. This can be done by inserting new lines into the program. Do this by typing:

```
15  PRINT FIRST
25  PRINT LAST
35  PRINT N
```

Note how each line fits neatly into the program after you press NEW LINE. Now give the RUN command so that you can check the program.

If you want to remove the extra lines again, just type in:

```
15
25
35
```

pressing NEW LINE after each number. If you then run the program, you will see that the lines have been removed. This illustrates the general principle that any line can be deleted from a program by typing the number of that particular line followed by NEW LINE.

Now experiment with error correction by deliberately typing an error in the program.

```
2Ø  LET LEST=1ØØ
```

Note that the original line has now been replaced by the new line and the name LAST has been replaced by LEST. This also illustrates an effective method of correcting errors: type the number of the line to be altered, followed by the correct instruction.

It is, of course, interesting to know whether a program actually contains an incorrigible error. Give the command:

RUN (followed by NEW LINE)

Instead of the correct answer, the screen will display an error report, which in this case will read:

```
2/4Ø
```

The second number, the number 40, indicates the number of

the line in which the mistake was found during the running of the program. The first number, the number 2, indicates the type of error. In Appendix A you can check this error report. Code 2 means that a variable is being used in an expression without having first been given a value.

Type NEW LINE again or give the LIST command. In either case the program will reappear. Line 40 contains the variable LAST, which has not yet been given a value as the value 100 was assigned to the variable LEST, a different variable altogether, in the deliberately incorrect line 20.

In this case there are two ways of correcting the error. You could replace the name LAST in line 40 by LEST, more sensibly, you could replace LEST in line 20 by LAST. Correct the error by again typing:

```
20  LET LAST=100
```

There is however another method that will in many cases be preferable. This method is based on direct cursor control. Have a look at the arrows on the keyboard above the 5, 6, 7, and 8 keys. With the up-arrow and the down-arrow you can move the program cursor up or down. You can try this out, but don't forget to press SHIFT while typing 6 or 7. By moving the cursor up or down you can select a particular line. Make sure that you move the cursor so that it is pointing to line 20. Then type in:

EDIT (using SHIFT and 1)

and the line indicated by the cursor will appear at the bottom of the screen so that it can be edited. The cursor at the bottom of the screen can now be moved by means of the right-arrow and the left-arrow (above the 5 and 8 keys). Try this as well. The cursor should then be moved to the right of the error; in other words, the display on your screen should look like Fig. 6-1.

Now type:

RUBOUT (using SHIFT and 0)

and then type in the correct letter.

Then type NEW LINE again and the program is completed.

You will have noticed that RUBOUT caused a symbol to be deleted. It is possible to rub out a number of symbols by pressing

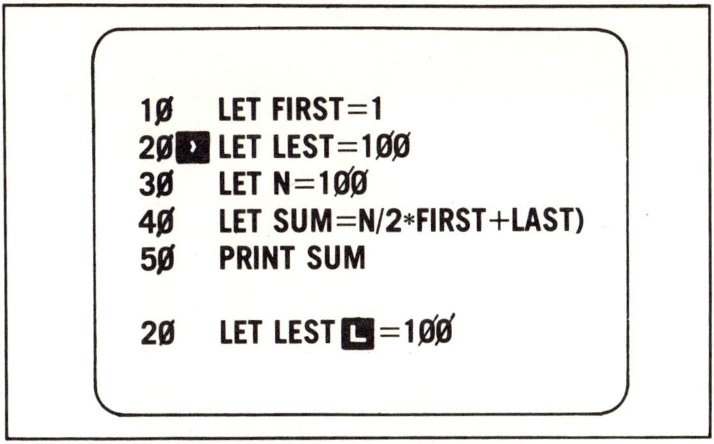

Fig. 6-1. Direct cursor control and EDIT can be used for correcting errors.

RUBOUT repeatedly (holding down the SHIFT key, of course). This method must always be used if an error is made during the typing of a line and the error is immediately recognized by the computer (a syntax error). Type, for example:

```
5Ø  PRINT + SUM
```

The + sign does not belong there, and the computer will show this by displaying the S cursor to the left of the wrong symbol. This cursor will not appear on the screen until NEW LINE is pressed. In this case it is impossible to include the line in the program by pressing NEW LINE. Typing NEW LINE at this point does not have any effect other than making the S cursor appear: the ZX81 demands that the discovered error is corrected before you do anything else. Again, correct the error by moving the cursor to the spot where the eror occurred. The + sign can then be removed by pressing TUBOUT and the line can be added to the program by pressing NEW LINE.

The up-arrow and the down-arrow can also be used when you are studying a program listing. This is especially useful when a program is so large that it cannot be displayed on the screen in its entirety. By pressing the down-arrow the lines with the higher line numbers are shown, and by pressing the up-arrow the lines with lower line numbers will appear.

Chapter 7

Using the Computer as a Calculator

Up to this point, the ZX81 has been regarded mainly as a machine that can execute programs, but it also enables the user to give instructions that do not have a line number. Such instructions are commands and enable the ZX81 owner to use the computer as a calculator.

Here is an example. Type:

```
PRINT 5.341*6.7
```

Then type NEW LINE, and the computer will immediately give the answer.

```
35.7847
```

It would also have been possible to carry out this calculation as a program, and this illustration will demonstrate that there is a marked difference.

First, clear the memory by giving the NEW command. Then type in the "microprogram," starting with a line number.

```
10  PRINT 5.341*6.7
```

The answer will not appear until the RUN command is given, so type RUN and the answer will appear again, with the message Ø/1Ø displayed at the bottom of the screen. Every time you give the RUN command the answer will appear again. This is not possible with the first example, using the computer as a calculator. A command, such as PRINT 5.341*6.7 is forgotten once it has been executed.

A PRINT command, as in this example, can obviously include an arithmetic expression, in this case multiplication

The following example shows that you can also execute a series of direct commands. First, clear the memory by giving the NEW command. Then type in the following sequence. Each line must be followed by NEW LINE, which apparently causes that line to be erased.

```
LET A=1
LET B=2
LET C=A+B
PRINT C
```

As soon as the last line has been typed, the answer will appear as the "instructions" were not preceded by line numbers, therefore each line was treated as a command. The computer has not forgotten everything, however, Just type in:

```
PRINT B
```

and the computer will give the answer 2. This facility can be put to good use when you want to trace errors in a program. Such PRINT commands (that is, PRINT commands not preceded by line numbers) provide you with a simple method of checking the values of different variables when a program has been run.

The ZX81 is also provided with a separate command—the command CLEAR—for erasing the values assigned to all variables. If you give this command and then type PRINT B, an error report indicates that the variable B is unknown.

The CLEAR command can also be useful when tracing errors. The fact that, as a result of alterations in the program, certain instructions are no longer being carried out, might escape your notice, despite the execution of direct PRINT commands. The reason for this is that the variables may have been given a value earlier on. By using CLEAR you can prevent this difficulty as all variables are deleted. The CLEAR command can also be used to release storage space occupied by variables.

All instructions except the INPUT instruction can be used as commands, but in practice you will find that it is chiefly the direct PRINT command that is important, particularly when it comes to tracing errors in programs. After all, we do not buy a computer with the intention of using it solely as a calculator. The best thing to feed into a computer is definitely a program.

Chapter 8

The LET Instruction

In every program discussed so far, we have used the LET instruction. Without doubt this is one of the most common BASIC instructions and it is therefore important to understand its use.

With an instruction such as:

```
30  LET N=100
```

the = sign does not mean "is equal to" (in the sense N equals 100). The instruction is best translated by "N becomes 100" or "N will be given the value 100." It is therefore advisable always to refer to the = sign in a LET instruction as the "becomes" sign. This is clearly illustrated by the following instruction:

```
30  LET N=N+100
```

According to the rules of algebra, the expression N=N+100 is nonsense (it is called a "conflicting equation"). In BASIC it is an expression indicating that the new value of N will be obtained by adding 100 to the old value. If this were followed by an instruction such as:

```
60 LET N=40
```

the old value would be cancelled and would be replaced by the new value 40.

LET is always followed by the name of a variable, the = sign, and a value or an expression that will yield a value.

With many versions of BASIC you can omit LET. For example, you could write:

```
40 N=100
```

This is not possible with the ZX81. This knowledge may be useful if you want to translate existing BASIC programs into ZX81 BASIC. Whenever you see: "line number variable = expression," you need to insert LET after the line number.

With other versions of BASIC it is also possible to write more than one instruction on one line separated by the : sign. With ZX81 BASIC this is not possible. Instructions should be typed on separate lines. Some BASICS also do not allow spaces before or after keywords such as LET, in order to save storage space. On the ZX81 spaces are automatically put in when a keyword is typed in. This is very useful as the spaces help to make the program readable.

Chapter 9
The INPUT, PRINT, and REM Instructions

Before discussing these instructions, here is a reminder of the program prepared to find the sum of the terms of a series. The program is:

```
1Ø  LET FIRST=1
2Ø  LET LAST=1ØØ
3Ø  LET N=1ØØ
4Ø  LET SUM=N/2*(FIRST+LAST)
5Ø  PRINT SUM
```

THE INPUT INSTRUCTION

This is not a general program, it calculates the sum of the terms of one particular series. The method used, however, can be used for any series in which every term is found by adding a constant to the previous term (an arithmetic series). The program could therefore be re-used if the user could simply type in the value of the first term, the last term and the number of terms, without having to alter the program. This is made possible by the INPUT instructions which always takes the form: "INPUT name of variable."

Such an INPUT instruction causes a temporary interruption in the running of the program. The user must then type in a value (followed by NEW LINE) and this value will be assigned to the variable indicated. When you have typed in the INPUT instructions, the example will look like this:

```
10  INPUT FIRST
20  INPUT LAST
30  INPUT N
40  LET SUM=N/2*(FIRST+LAST)
50  PRINT SUM
```

Experiment with these alterations.

Run the program. The screen will go blank except for the L cursor, which will appear in the bottom left-hand corner. This means that you must input a number, or an expression. For example, if you input the expression 1*4+3/7, the computer will evaluate this expression first. For the moment, use our original example. Type:

```
1
```

This is the input for "first." You will see the L cursor reappear immediately, so you need to input another number, a value for the variable LAST. Type:

```
100
```

The L cursor will reappear again, so you need to type in value for N:

```
100
```

and the familiar answer 5050 will appear again.

This program can now be used for other values, such as to find the sum of the first 50 values. First enter RUN and then type in succession:

```
1
50
50
```

The computer will give the answer 1275. This demonstrates that the general usefulness of the program has improved considerably.

The program does, however, have another obvious shortcoming. A programmer would say that it is not very "user-friendly." A program that is "user-friendly" can be run by the user without his having any previous knowledge of the program. In this case, however, a lot of previous knowledge is necessary. You need to know in advance that you must first input a number representing the value of the variable FIRST, and so on.

THE PRINT INSTRUCTION

To avoid this problem, you can include messages in the program. It is possible to print text by using the PRINT instruction, provided the text is enclosed in quotation marks. Below you will see an improved version of the original program. For clarity the original line numbers are unchanged. The numbers of the additional lines end in 5. You can carry out these alterations yourself. Note that spaces in the text inside quotation marks are typed in by pressing SPACE.

```
 5  PRINT "INPUT FIRST"
1Ø  INPUT FIRST
15  PRINT "INPUT LAST"
2Ø  INPUT LAST
25  PRINT "INPUT NUMBER OF TERMS"
3Ø  INPUT N
4Ø  LET SUM=N/*(FIRST+LAST)
45  PRINT "THE SUM IS"
5Ø  PRINT SUM
```

Note that line 25 takes up two lines on the screen. When you start the program you will first see the text:

```
INPUT FIRST
```

The quotation marks have disappeared. Then type in a value.

You can also give several messages in one PRINT statement:

```
5Ø  PRINT "THE SUM";SUM
```

If you carry out this alteration you should of course delete line 45. The two items that will now be printed are the text THE SUM IS and the value of the variable SUM. As these two are separated in the PRINT statement by a semicolon, (;) one is printed (,) immediately after the other. If instead of the semicolon you had used a comma, the computer would have placed the value of SUM in a subsequent column as the computer automatically divides the screen into two columns if you type a comma. This PRINT statement includes two items to be printed. In practice you can include more items separated by the ; and , signs.

The ; and , signs can also occur as the final symbol in a PRINT instruction. Any item to be printed will then immediately follow the text already printed (in the case of a ;) or be placed in the next column (in the case of a ,).

An empty PRINT instruction causes the program to include a blank line.

The preceding points can be illustrated by the following program:

```
40  LET SUM=45
50  PRINT "THE SUM",
60  PRINT "IS"
70  PRINT
80  PRINT "THE NUMBER":
90  PRINT SUM
```

The result will be:

```
THE SUM          IS    (text in 2 columns)
                       (blank line)
THE NUMBER 45          (45 immediately follows the text)
```

The PRINT statement in BASIC is simple in structure. The following guidelines should be useful.

1. More than one item can be printed if the items are separated by ; or ,. Use a ; if you want the items to follow each other. Use a , if you want the second item placed in a subsequent column. If there is not enough room for a second column, the item will be placed at the beginning of a new line.
2. If a PRINT statement ends in ; the next text to be printed will immediately follow the previous item.
3. If a PRINT statement ends in , the next test to be printed will be placed in a subsequent column.

4. In a PRINT statement, text is always enclosed in quotation marks. PRINT by itself causes the program to skip a line.
5. A PRINT statement can include an expression that has yet to be evaluated. This was demonstrated in Chapter 7 when dealing with the direct PRINT instructions.

THE REM INSTRUCTION

It is sometimes helpful to include additional information in a program in the form of directions that are important only to the programmer. Such information could, for instance, refer to the method of solving a problem and is not intended to appear on the screen during the running of the program. Consequently it should only be displayed in program listings.

These directions can be included in the program by placing the keyword REM (for "remark") at the beginning of the line. Below you see the final program, complete with REM "statements." The original line numbers remain unchanged.

```
 1  REM PROGRAM TO FIND THE SUM
 2  REM OF AN ARITHMETICAL SERIES
 3  REM ACCORDING TO FORMULA
 4  REM SUM=N/2*(FIRST+LAST)
 5  PRINT "INPUT FIRST"
1Ø  INPUT FIRST
15  PRINT "INPUT LAST"
2Ø  INPUT LAST
25  PRINT "INPUT NUMBER OF TERMS"
3Ø  INPUT N
4Ø  LET SUM=N/2*(FIRST+LAST)
5Ø  PRINT "THE SUM IS ";SUM
```

If your computer only has 1K RAM memory, you will have to be very economical with REM statements as the memory will fill up very quickly. If your computer has sufficient memory space, however, it is better to use frequent REM statements. This is, in fact, one of the best methods of documentation. By using REM statements, you can be certain that the documentation cannot be lost during programming.

Chapter 10
The TAB, AT, CLS, and SCROLL Instructions

This chapter deals with some other facts concerning printing or the displaying of certain values or symbols on the screen.

THE TAB INSTRUCTION

You have already seen how to use a comma or a semicolon to tell the computer where to print a given item. BASIC offers another standard feature in the form of the TAB instruction. The effect of this instruction is the same as that of the tabulator or tab function on a typewriter.

An example of a TAB instruction can be seen in the following expression:

```
10  PRINT TAB 11;"CHAPTER 1"
```

As a result of this instruction, the text CHAPTER 1 will start at the 11th position on the line. Note the notation: TAB is immediately followed by the specified character position. With most versions of BASIC the character position after TAB must always be placed within brackets. In this case a number is given to indicate the column. It is also possible for TAB to be followed by a variable. The value of the variable will then indicate the position of the column.

By using the TAB instruction you can also draw dotted lines on the screen. The following program shows how this is done:

```
10 PRINT TAB 1;"X"
20 PRINT TAB 2;"X"
30 PRINT TAB 3;"X"
40 PRINT TAB 4;"X"
50 PRINT TAB 5;""""
```

The result of this program is a dotted line:

```
X
 X
  X
   X
    X
```

The possibility of drawing lines can be exploited further by using the FOR...NEXT instruction, which we shall discuss in Chapter 14.

The TAB instruction will be found under the P key. On the ZX81 the terms under the keys are functions. Before typing such a function you must first press the FUNCTION key (that is, shifted NEW LINE). The cursor will show the letter F (for FUNCTION) to indicate that the next key to be pressed will be interpreted as a function. If you then press P, TAB will automatically appear on the screen.

> NEVER FORGET:
>
> A term under a key can be typed by first pressing shifted NEW LINE (the cursor will then show F for FUNCTION) and then pressing the appropriate key.

THE AT INSTRUCTION

The ZX81 contains another very powerful instruction, called the AT instruction, with which you can control the printing position and print an item anywhere on the screen. AT is always followed by two numbers separated by a comma. These numbers indicate the line and the position on the line where the next item is to be printed.

As an exercise, try the following program:

```
10  PRINT "INTPUT X"
20  INPUT X
30  PRINT "INPUT Y"
40  INPUT Y
50  PRINT AT X,Y;"X"
```

It is also possible to overwrite existing text with the AT instruction. Try 0, 0. This AT instruction is especially useful when constructing all kinds of graphic representations, such as designing games. Just as TAB, AT is written under a key, the C key. This means that before typing AT you must press FUNCTION (shifted NEW LINE).

THE CLS AND SCROLL INSTRUCTIONS

Sometimes you may want to clear the entire screen in one step. This can be done by using the CLS, or clear screen, instruction, using the V key followed by NEW LINE. Try typing:

```
CLS
```

and you will see that the screen is immediately cleared.

CLS can also be included in a program as an instruction, just as the final instruction to be discussed in this chapter, the SCROLL instruction. If the screen is displaying text, the SCROLL instruction will move the whole display up one line, causing the top line to disappear from the screen.

Chapter 11
About Numbers

Despite the fact that computers are capable of doing a great deal more than simply carrying out calculations, arithmetic remains one of the most important fields of application. Arithmetic uses numbers, and this chapter will examine the ways in which numbers can be represented.

First of all there are *integers*. These are the whole numbers 0, 1, 2, 3, etc., as well as −1, −2, −3, etc. The term "etc.", of course, has its limitations, as in view of the limited storage space for numbers, any sequence must have a lowest and a highest number specified. For the ZX81 these numbers are 4294967295 and −4294967296 respectively. In absolute terms these are large numbers, but there are calculations for which they are inadequate. Just think of astronomy, where it is usual to work with very large numbers.

In addition to whole numbers, there is of course a need for numbers containing a *decimal point*, so that the division 1/2 gives the answer 0.5 and not 0 or 1.

For clarity, here is a checklist of the main groups.

1. Whole numbers, or integers from −4294967296 to 4294967295.

2. Decimal numbers, or real numbers, such as 0.5 or –4.7304.
3. Numbers that can represent very high and very low values. These numbers are written in scientific notation.

The first two categories are more straightforward and will be dealt with here, the last category will be dealt with at the end of the chapter.

One rule of BASIC is that as long as a variable is a whole number, it is stored as such. As soon as a calculation results in a decimal number, a different kind of notation is used in the memory. This will not be apparent to the user. In a number of cases it is better to replace a decimal number by the nearest whole number. For this purpose BASIC has the following function: INT, which stands for integer, a whole number.

In the next chapter, the term *function* will be dealt with in detail. At this point it is sufficient to say that a function is simply a rule for giving one number in exchange for another. The function "the square of," for example, is a rule that changes 3 to 9. The rule is: multiply the number by itself.

The following example program illustrates the INT function.

```
10  LET A=2.7
20  LET B=INT(A)
30  LET C=INT(A+0.5)
40  PRINT "INT(2.7)=";B
50  PRINT "INT(2.7+0.5)=";C
```

The result of this program is:

```
INT(2.7)=2
INT(2.7+0.5)=3
```

In line 10 the real value 2.7 is assigned to A. In line 20 variable B is given the value we get by applying the INT function to A (2.7). The result is the number obtained by rounding down to the nearest integer or whole number. Thus B will be given the integer value 2 and the PRINT instruction in line 40 will confirm this. In line 30 the value INT(2.7 + 0.5) is assigned to C. When the value 0.5 is added to 2.7, the result, 3.2, is then rounded down to the nearest whole number. This is the method by which any number above .5 of a decimal point can be rounded to the nearest whole number. Thus 2.7 + 0.5 is rounded to 3.

REMEMBER:
A number A can be rounded by using the expression INT (A + 0.5)

With negative numbers this can create problems. It is important to note that the INT function is interpreted differently in some versions of BASIC. It is essential not to copy other BASIC programs indiscriminately. The following example illustrates what happens on the ZX81.

```
PRINT INT(–3.1)
```

gives –4.

This shows once again that on the ZX81 the INT function rounds down to the smaller whole number.

With some arithmetic problems it is not the size of the number that is important; rather it is the sign. There are three possible signs.

1. The number is negative. In this case the number is preceded by the – sign.
2. The number is positive. In this case the number is not usually preceded by a sign (on the ZX81 this is not possible), but the + sign is implied.
3. The number does not have a sign. Only the number 0 is in this unique position.

The sign of a number, expressed as the value –1, 1, or 0, can be found by using the SGN, or sign, function. This is illustrated by the following program:

```
10 LET A=–2.7
20 LET B=2.7
30 LET C=0
40 LET AS=SGN(A)
50 LET BS=SGN(B)
60 LET CS=SGN(C)
70 PRINT "AS=";AS
80 PRINT "BS=";BS
90 PRINT "CS=";CS
```

The result of this program is:

```
AS=-1
BA=1
CS=Ø
```

Lines 10, 20, 30, 70, 80, and 90 should not present any problems. In lines 40, 50, and 60 the SGN function is used. AS is given the value SGN(A). The value of A is −2.7, therefore the SGN function of A is −1. Similarly BS becomes 1 and CS becomes 0.

The final subject to be dealt with in this chapter is very large and very small numbers. Consider the number 56 540 000 000 000 000. This is literally an astronomical number. It could conceivably represent the distance between some heavenly body and the Earth. Such a number cannot be typed into the ZX81 simply as a number. To overcome this problem a notation is used by which each number can be represented as a number multiplied by a power of 10.

Take, for example, 5654×10^{13}. The first number, 5654, is called the *mantissa*, and the second, 10^{13}, is called the *exponent*. On the ZX81, the figures must always be typed neatly on one line. The number 13, which in a book can be positioned to the right of and above the 10, must therefore be written differently in BASIC. The convention is simple. First type the mantissa, then the letter E and finally the power of 10, the exponent. Our example; 5654×10^{13} would be typed as:

```
5654E13
```

The same procedure is followed in the case of very small numbers, 0.0000000000005654, for example. This is the same as 5654×10^{-13} and is therefore typed on the computer as:

```
5654E-13
```

Remember that this is an entirely correct way of writing numbers and that numbers can therefore be entered in this notation after an INPUT instruction. In order to gain some experience, try out the following program several times, using different numbers:

```
1Ø  INPUT A
2Ø  INPUT B
3Ø  PRINT A*B
```

Chapter 12

Numerical Functions

On a scientific calculator, there are many terms referring to the so-called scientific functions. The calculator in fact already contains a number of standard programs for calculating the various functions. The ZX81, too, contains standard programs for the calculation of different functions. The standard programs are stored in the ROM.

Before discussing the notation of functions, it is essential to understand the notions function and argument. In general terms, a *function* is a rule or prescription for changing one number to a different number. In the case of the square root function, the rule is: the square root of a certain value is the number which, when multiplied by itself, yields the original value. According to this rule the square root of 9 is the value 3, as 3 × 3 gives the value 9. The number that is converted by the function is called the *argument* and the value obtained is the result of the function.

Generally speaking, BASIC uses the following notation for functions: name of function (argument). For instance:

```
SQR(9)
```

Here the term SQR is the name of the function (square root)

and 9 is the argument of the function. In other words, $\sqrt{9}$ is written SQR(9) in BASIC. When you give the direct PRINT instruction:

```
PRINT SQR(9)
```

the value 3 will be the result.

On the ZX81 the parentheses can be omitted, provided the argument is a simple number and not an expression. It is best to use parentheses, however, as the use of parentheses follows standard BASIC and also prevents any misunderstandings, especially with more complicated expressions. For example:

```
PRINT SQR(2+SQR(16+9)+4/2)
```

would result in a different answer with and without brackets.

This example also shows that the argument of a function can be an expression that is still to be evaluated. It can also include other functions and variables. The result is usually calculated to an accuracy of 8 digits.

On the ZX81 all function names are written underneath the keys. These terms can be typed in by first typing FUNCTION (shifted NEW LINE). The cursor will change to F to show that the computer expects the name of a function, and the function will be typed automatically on pressing the relevant key.

Table 12-1 provides a list of the functions. These are used mainly in scientific calculations and will therefore not be used by

Table 12-1. ZX81 Functions.

BASIC Name	Algebraic Notation	Meaning
SIN(X)	sin(x)	Gives the sine of x; x in radians.
COS(X)	cos(x)	Gives the cosine of x; x in radians.
TAN(X)	tan(x)	Gives the tangent of x; x in radians.
ASN(X)	arcsin(x)	Gives the arcsine; answer in radians.
ACS(X)	arccos(x)	Gives the arccosine; answer in radians.
ATN(X)	arctan(x)	Gives the arctangent; answer in radians.
LN(X)	eln(x)	Gives the natural logarithm of x.
EXP(X)	e^x	Gives e to the power of x.
SQR(X)	$\sqrt{x}$	Gives the square root of x.
ABS(X)	$\|x\|$	Gives the absolute value of x.
SGN(X)		Gives −1, 0, 1, dependent on the sign of x.
INT(X)		Rounds down x to nearest whole number.

many people. The SGN and INT functions in the list were discussed in Chapter 11.

Note that there is no separate function for raising one number to the power of another, EXP(X), whereas most scientific calculators do not have such a function. In BASIC you carry out this operation, for example 2^3, by using the symbol **. This symbol can be typed with a single keystroke, shifted H. For example,

```
PRINT 2**3
```

gives the value 2*2*2=8.

There are a few unusual functions that have no argument. Strictly speaking, they are therefore not true functions, but they will be treated as functions since their names are written underneath the keys on the keyboard and they can only be called up when FUNCTION is pressed first.

The PI, or π function immediately gives the value π, that is the value 3.141592653. The computer actually stores 10 digits of this number, but only 8 are displayed. The symbol π is, in fact, written under the M key, but the screen always displays the letters PI.

The RND function gives a random number between 0 and 1. It can take the value 0, but never the value 1. This function is especially useful in games, as it is the function that introduces an unpredictable element.

The term RND is written under the T key. Above this key you will see RAND. You can use RAND to "shake the bag of random numbers" so that the RND function does not always give the same "random" numbers. The ZX81 contains a sequence of 65536 random numbers. After 65536 "draws" we get the same sequence again, so the numbers are not totally random. The RAND statement, which always takes the form "RAND number", indicates the place where the RND function will start to select random numbers from the given sequence.

Special attention should be given to the expression:

RAND Ø (or RAND, they are identical)

In this case the length of time the television has been switched on determines the place where RND is to start reading the random numbers. This usually yields genuinely random numbers. For a practical demonstration, try running the following programs a number of times, running the second program with different, fairly long intervals.

```
10  REM PROGRAM LOADED DICE
20  RAND 1
30  LET RESULT=INT((RND*6)+1.)
40  PRINT RESULT
```

and

```
10  REM PROGRAM DICE
20  RAND 0
30  LET RESULT=INT((RND*6)+1.)
40  PRINT RESULT
```

Note how in line 30 RESULT is given an arbitrary number between 1 and 6, by means of the expression:

```
INT((RND*6)+1.)
```

If N represents an integer you can obtain a random number between 1 and N (including 1 and N) by using the expression:

```
INT((RND*N)+1.)
```

This may be interesting for those who intend to write their own games.

Chapter 13
The IF...THEN, GOTO, STOP, AND, OR, NOT, CONT, and BREAK Instructions

The programs discussed so far have always been designed in such a way that the solution to a problem was found by carrying out a series of instructions one by one, from beginning to end.

THE IF...THEN INSTRUCTION

Suppose that in the course of writing a program you enter three values relating to the lengths of the three sides of a triangle. With the set of instructions at your disposal, it is difficult to decide on the basis of the available information whether you are dealing with an isosceles triangle, in which at least two sides are equal. The most obvious method would be to ask questions such as, "Is the first side equal to the second?" If the answer is no; then ask, "Is the first side equal to the third?" If the answer is again no, then ask, "Is the second side equal to the third"? You would need instructions with which to ask these and similar questions.

BASIC contains a simple instruction that makes this possible, the IF...THEN instruction. The word IF is always followed by an expression that is either true or false. If the expression is true, the instruction given after THEN is executed. If the expression is false, the computer simply continues with the next line of the program. An example of an IF statement is:

```
IF SIDE1=SIDE2 THEN PRINT "ISOSCELES"
```

This means: IF SIDE 1 is equal to SIDE 2 THEN print the message ISOSCELES. In principle THEN can be followed by any instruction, including GOTO.

THE GOTO AND STOP INSTRUCTIONS

The GOTO instruction tells the computer to jump to a specified line number. The computer must then continue the program starting from the line indicated. The GOTO instruction always has the form: GOTO line number. For instance:

```
GOTO 40
```

The following program shows both the IF...THEN and the GOTO instructions. The program gives a solution to the problem mentioned at the beginning of this chapter, checking whether three values given for the three sides of a triangle show the triangle to be an isosceles.

```
 10 REM IDENTIFYING A TRIANGLE
 20 PRINT "INPUT SIDE 1"
 30 INPUT SIDE1
 40 PRINT "INPUT SIDE 2"
 50 INPUT SIDE2
 60 PRINT "INPUT SIDE 3"
 70 INPUT SIDE3
 80 IF SIDE1=SIDE2 THEN GOTO 130
 90 IF SIDE1=SIDE3 THEN GOTO 130
100 IF SIDE2=SIDE3 THEN GOTO 130
110 PRINT "NOT AN ISOSCELES"
120 STOP
130 PRINT "ISOSCELES"
```

The first line is a REM statement. This is followed by a PRINT instruction indicating that a number needs to be input. This number must refer to the first side of the triangle. By means of the INPUT instruction in line 30 this number is assigned to the variable SIDE 1.

In the same way the second and third numbers are assigned to SIDE 2 and SIDE 3 respectively.

Now the program has to do some thinking. Line 80 says:

```
IF SIDE1=SIDE2 THEN GOTO 13Ø
```

In other words, if side 1 is equal to side 2, the program jumps to line 130, skipping lines 90 to 120. Line 130 says:

```
PRINT "ISOSCELES"
```

In this case you get the message that the triangle is an isosceles, which is of course correct, as two sides were found to be equal.

If side 1 is not equal to side 2, the instruction following THEN will not be executed and the computer will continue with line 90, checking sides 1 and 3. The construction is in fact identical to the previous one. If side 1 and side 3 are not equal either, a final test will be executed, comparing sides 2 and 3.

If none of the IF...THEN instructions is followed by a jump—in other words in none of these cases is one side found to be equal to another side—then the obvious conclusion is that the triangle is not an isosceles, which is in fact the message we get as a result of the PRINT instruction in line 110.

But be careful at this point. If you do not take action, this would be followed by the message ISOSCELES. This problem can be solved by giving the STOP instruction in line 120. As the word indicates, this instruction stops the execution of the program. Now practice by running the program and try out various situations.

RELATIONS

In the previous program two values of variables are compared in each IF...THEN statement with the aid of the = sign. Here the = sign actually means "is equal to." It is also possible to ask questions such as "is side 1 greater than side 2" or "is side 1 less than or equal to side 2". In this case the > and < = signs are used. These signs are called relations: they show the relation between two values. In Table 13-1 you will find a list of the relations used on the ZX81.

You can see from your keyboard that each of these signs, including the signs consisting of more than one symbol, must be typed by pressing a single key, using SHIFT.

Table 13-1. ZX81 Signs That Show Relations between Two Values.

Sign	Meaning	Example
=	Equals	IF A=B THEN . . .
<	Less than	IF A<B THEN . . .
<=	Less than or equal to	IF A<=B THEN . . .
>	Greater than	IF A>B THEN . . .
>=	Greater than or equal to	IF A>=B THEN . . .
< >	Not equal to	IF A< >B THEN . . .

AND, OR, AND NOT

Have another look at the program identifying a triangle. It contains a succession of three similar IF statements. The program checks in fact whether side 1 = side 2, or side 1 = side 3, or side 2 = side 3 and if at least one of these relations is true we jump to the statement PRINT "ISOSCELES". BASIC enables us to express all this more briefly with the aid of the word OR. The expression:

SIDE1=SIDE2 OR SIDE1=SIDE3

is true if at least one of the relations is true. It is possible to combine more relations such as in

SIDE1=SIDE2 OR SIDE1=SIDE3 OR SIDE2=SIDE3

By using this expression you can considerably shorten the program for identifying a triangle.

In addition to the word OR, you can use the word AND. AND connects two relations and the combined expression is true only if both relations are true. So as a result of the statement:

```
IF A=1 AND B=2 THEN PRINT "A IS 1 AND B IS 2"
```

the PRINT instruction will be carried out only if A equals 1 and B equals 2. In all other cases the PRINT instruction is not executed.

The terms AND and OR can also be combined, using parentheses if required. For example:

```
(A=1 AND B=2) OR (A=2 AND B=3)
```

A diagram representing the meanings of the words AND and OR follows. In the diagram X and Y stand for relations that are true or false.

X	Y	X AND Y	X OR Y
true	true	true	true
true	false	false	true
false	true	false	true
false	false	false	false

The value of a relation can be changed by placing NOT in front of it. This is illustrated in the following diagram:

X	NOT X
true	false
false	true

Now experiment with this little game. You are standing on top of a tower and you are throwing objects down to the ground. According to the physical law the rate of fall is $V = \sqrt{2 \times 9.8 \times H}$, in which H represents the height of the tower. For practice, try out the program for yourself.

```
10 REM PISA GUESSING GAME
20 PRINT "INPUT HEIGHT TOWER"
30 INPUT H
```

```
 40  LET V=SQR (2*9.8*H)
 50  PRINT "WHAT IS THE RATE OF FALL?"
 60  INPUT VGUESS
 70  LET DIFFERENCE=ABS (V-VGUESS)
 80  IF DIFFERENCE<1 THEN GOTO 110
 90  PRINT "YOU ARE WRONG . . ."
100  GOTO 50
110  PRINT "CORRECT"
```

CONTINUE OR INTERRUPT

The final subjects to be discussed are the CONT and BREAK commands. By using the CONT command you can continue a program after it has been interrupted, for example by a STOP instruction. The following short program hardly needs any explanation.

```
10  PRINT "A"
20  STOP
30  PRINT "B"
40  STOP
50  PRINT "C"
```

The result is as follows:

RUN (followed by NEW LINE to start the program)

```
A       (after this the program is interrupted)
CONT
B       (after this the program is interrupted again)
CONT
C
```

If during the running of a program the screen is completely filled, the computer will interrupt the program and error report 5 (see page 102) will appear. By typing CONT you can then continue the program. Naturally the screen will automatically be cleared first.

REMEMBER: If the screen is full . . . use CONT.

With the BREAK command you can interrupt the running of a program. Consider for instance the following short program:

```
10  GOTO 20
20  GOTO 10
```

When you start the program, the computer will first jump to line 20, and having arrived there, it will jump back to line 10, then back to line 20, and so on. This is described as an "endless loop". Of course you could now disconnect the machine to break the loop, but the program would be lost as a result. This particular program is useless, but in practice such a loop occasionally occurs in a relatively large program. In this case you can give the BREAK command. Error report D will then appear on the screen as will the number of the line in which the BREAK action occurred.

This command is also useful when you use a cassette recorder. If the controls are not adjusted properly, this can be corrected by using the BREAK command. The use of a cassette recorder is discussed in more detail in Chapter 19.

Chapter 14

The FOR...NEXT Instruction

Everybody has at some time worked out an average: average age, average distance, average gasoline consumption, and so on. You find the average of a series of numbers by adding up all the numbers, then dividing the total by the number of items.

Suppose you wanted to find the average of 5 numbers using the computer. You could do this with the aid of the following program:

```
 1Ø  LET SUM=Ø
 2Ø  INPUT NUMBER1
 3Ø  LET SUM=SUM+NUMBER1
 4Ø  INPUT NUMBER2
 5Ø  LET SUM=SUM+NUMBER2
 6Ø  INPUT NUMBER3
 7Ø  LET SUM=SUM+NUMBER3
 8Ø  INPUT NUMBER4
 9Ø  LET SUM=SUM+NUMBER4
1ØØ  INPUT NUMBERS
11Ø  LET SUM=SUM+NUMBER5
12Ø  LET AVERAGE=SUM/5
13Ø  PRINT AVERAGE
```

This is clearly a bad program as it is inflexible. It is suitable for a short series, and it is very long. It would be totally impractical to use this program to find the average of 100 numbers.

With the aid of the IF...THEN instruction, you can overcome all these problems. The following is a version of the program that is very user-friendly:

```
10  REM PROGRAM AVERAGE
20  PRINT "INPUT NUMBER OF VALUES"
30  INPUT NUMBER OF VALUES
40  LET N=1
50  LET SUM=0
60  PRINT "INPUT NUMBER NO";N;"
70  INPUT NUMBER
80  LET SUM=SUM+NUMBER
90  LET N=N+1
100 IF N<= NUMBER OF ITEMS THEN GOTO 60
110 LET AVERAGE=SUM/NUMBER OF VALUES
120 PRINT "AVERAGE=";AVERAGE
```

Lines 10, 20, and 30 do not present any problems. Line 30 asks for the number of items of which the average must be calculated, making the program suitable for a series of any length. In lines 40 and 50 two initial values are assigned: N is given the initial value 1, and SUM is given the inital value 0. With N you keep a record of the number of values that have been input. SUM will add each new number to the total. Thus SUM will finally contain the total of all the numbers you have input.

This practice of assigning an initial value is very common in programming, so it will be helpful to study it very carefully. Lines 60, 70, 80, 90, and 100 form a complete unit, which will be executed repeatedly for as long as N is less than or equal to the number of items. Such a unit is referred to as a "loop". The IF statement in line 100 checks whether all the numbers have been input. If this is not the case, the program returns to line 60, and the loop is executed once more. When the entire series has been input line 110 calculates the average by dividing SUM by the number of values. The result will finally be displayed in response to the PRINT instruction. Try running the program using the numbers 12, 10, 9, 13, and 11. The result should be 11.

In this program a series of instructions was executed a number of times, while the number was checked by means of a "control variable" (the variable N). N ran successively through the values 1, 2, 3, and so on, the number of values. This type of construction occurs so frequently that BASIC contains a special instruction to make it easier: the FOR...NEXT instruction. It is always structured: FOR name of variable-initial value TO limit. For instance:

```
FOR N=1 TO NUMBER OF VALUES
```

This is followed by the instructions that must be executed for all values of the "control variable" (the variable N in the preceding program). It is of course necessary to state which is to be the final instruction of the loop, in other words, the series of instructions which must be carried out repeatedly. After the final instruction of the loop, the program is to show the "flag": NEXT name of variable. For instance:

```
NEXT N
```

This can be illustrated again with the aid of the program AVERAGE, which will now include the FOR...NEXT instruction.

```
 10  REM PROGRAM AVERAGE
 20  PRINT "INPUT NUMBER OF VALUES"
 30  INPUT NUMBER OF VALUES
 40  LET SUM=0
 50  FOR N=1 TO NUMBER OF VALUES
 60  PRINT "INPUT NUMBER NO";N;"
 70  INPUT NUMBER
 80  LET SUM=SUM+NUMBER
 90  NEXT N
100  LET AVERAGE=SUM/NUMBER OF VALUES
110  PRINT "AVERAGE=";AVERAGE
```

Notice how easy this version is to read. Remember that the word TO in a FOR...NEXT statement must be typed by pressing the appropriate key (shifted A) so do not type T and O.

The FOR...NEXT instruction can be expanded by stating explicitly by what steps the control variable named after FOR is to go up, or down if the step value given is negative, each time. This can be demonstrated with the aid of a short program.

```
10  REM STEP DEMONSTRATION
```

```
20  FOR X=Ø.3 TO 6.8 STEP Ø.3
30  PRINT X
40  NEXT X
50  PRINT "END OF DEMONSTRATION"
```

Note that STEP 0.3 has been added to the FOR...NEXT statement. X will now have the values 0.3, 0.6, 0.9, and so on successively. The final value of X will be 6.6, as this would be followed by the value 6.6 = 0.3 = 6.9, which would be greater than the limit 6.8. If the STEP 0.3 part is omitted, the program automatically uses STEP 1, as the program AVERAGE showed. Use the appropriate key, SHIFT and E, to type STEP and do not type S, T, E, and P.

Here are a few more remarks concerning the FOR...NEXT instruction.

1. The variable following FOR is usually called the control variable. On the ZX81 the name of the control variable must consist of a single letter.
2. The initial value, limit, and step can also be given as expressions.
3. You must not jump into the middle of a FOR...NEXT loop from outside by using a GOTO instruction.
4. A FOR...NEXT loop can itself contain another FOR ...NEXT loop. FOR...NEXT loops must never overlap. This is illustrated by the following example.

Correct program	**Incorrect program**
FOR K=1 TO 20	FOR K=1 TO 20
. . .	. . .
FOR J=1 TO 10	FOR J=1 TO 10
. . .	. . .
. . .	. . .
NEXT J	NEXT K
. . .	. . .
NEXT K	NEXT J

The next program can be used to display a function on the screen. This is known as *plotting*. The function in this program is the sine function. Try this program and see if you understand how it works. A few REM statements have been included in the program to help you. Remember that PI is marked on the keyboard by the symbol π.

```
10 REM PLOTTING PROGRAM
20 FOR K=0 TO 2*PI STEP 2*PI/20
30 LET V=SIN(K)
40 REM NOW MOVE ON AND INCREASE
50 LET POS=(V+1)*10+1
60 REM NOW ROUND
70 LET POS=INT(POS+0.5)
80 PRINT TAB POS;"*"
90 NEXT K
```

When typing in lines 30, 40, and 50 you should remember that a sine always has a value between −1 and 1.

Chapter 15
Arrays

Starting again with a list of numbers, imagine that you now want to write a program to discover whether the list includes at least two numbers that are the same. It could happen that the first and last numbers are the same, which would mean that you would have to store the first number until the last number is input. The same would apply to the second and third numbers, and so on. Thus you need to store each number separately. But is it really necessary to use this awkward program?

```
10  INPUT NUMBER1
20  INPUT NUMBER2
30  INPUT NUMBER3
        etc.
```

It would certainly be unwieldy when dealing with a relatively long list of numbers.

Fortunately BASIC offers a very elegant solution for this problem in the form of an *array*. By using an array you can introduce a number of variables (as many as the available memory allows) with the aid of a single instruction. All these variables may then be treated as ordinary variables. Once you understand arrays in general, you can look for a solution to the preceding problem.

The instruction used to introduce the variables is called the DIM instruction. On the ZX81 it always looks like this: DIM letter (number). For instance:

```
DIM A(20)
```

In this case you can use the variables:

```
A(1), A(2), A(3), ... A(20)
```

All these variables A(1) to A(20) together form the array. As we have already pointed out, these variables can be used in the same way as any other variables. So the following expressions could all be used:

```
LET SUM=A(1)+24
LET A(2)=A(2)+SQR(A(4))
LET A(4)=A(3)**2+A(19)
```

The letter (in this case A) is called the *name*, and the number in brackets is the *subscript*. The subscript can also be represented indirectly by a variable or even by an expression. There are, therefore, three possibilities:

A(3)	(Subscript represented directly by a number)
A(K)	Subscript represented indirectly by a variable)
A(K + 4)	Subscript represented indirectly by an expression)

This is demonstrated in the following program:

```
10  DIM X(10)
20  FOR K=1 TO 10
30  LET X(K)=100+K
40  PRINT K,X(K)
50  NEXT K
60  LET SUM=X(1)+X(10)
70  PRINT "SUM=";SUM
```

This program gives the following result:

```
  1          1Ø1
  2          1Ø2
  3          1Ø3
  4          1Ø4
  5          1Ø5
  6          1Ø6
  7          1Ø7
  8          1Ø8
  9          1Ø9
 1Ø          11Ø
 SUM=211
```

In line 10 the DIM instruction reserves space for 10 variables. On the ZX81 the name of an array must be a single letter, which in this case is the letter X. In this way the variables X(1), X(2) ... X(10) are introduced. Line 20 is the start of a FOR...NEXT instruction. In line 30 the value 100 + K is assigned to the variable X(K). Thus the variable X(1) will first of all (K = 1) be given the value 100 + 1. Then the value of X(K) will be printed. In this way the loop (lines 30 and 40) will be executed 10 times, and values will be assigned to the variables X(1) to X(10) in the manner indicated. You can check this for yourself by using the PRINT instruction.

The FOR...NEXT instruction is followed by the instruction:

```
6Ø  LET SUM=X(1)+X(1Ø)
```

The subsequent PRINT instruction demonstrates that the computer has remembered the values X(1) and X(10).

Now to go back to the original problem: to find out whether a list of numbers contains at least two numbers that are the same. A series of numbers is input by using the FOR...NEXT instruction, discussed in Chapter 14.

```
1Ø  PRINT "INPUT NUMBER OF VALUES"
2Ø  INPUT NUMBER OF VALUES
3Ø  DIM A(NUMBER OF VALUES)
4Ø  FOR K=1 TO NUMBER OF VALUES
5Ø  PRINT "INPUT NUMBER NO";K;"
6Ø  INPUT A(K)
7Ø  NEXT K
```

This part should not present any further problems. Notice how in line 30 space is reserved for the variables A(1), A(2) to A(NUMBER OF VALUES). By means of the following FOR...NEXT instruction, each variable is given a value.

To discover whether at least two of the numbers are the same, you could start with the first number, A(1), and compare it successively with A(2), A(3), to A(NUMBER OF ITEMS). If these comparisons show two numbers to be the same, you can jump to a PRINT statement, which will print the message TWO NUMBERS ARE EQUAL. If this is not the case, you can forget about the first number and repeat the entire procedure with the second number. If this, too, should prove unsuccessful, you abandon the second number and repeat the procedure with the third number, and so on. All this can be expressed briefly in two FOR...NEXT statements.

```
 8Ø  FOR K=1 TO NUMBER OF VALUES
 9Ø  FOR J=K+1 TO NUMBER OF VALUES
1ØØ  IF A(K)=A(J) THEN GOTO 15Ø
11Ø  NEXT J
12Ø  NEXT K
13Ø  PRINT "NO TWO NUMBERS ARE EQUAL"
14Ø  STOP
15Ø  PRINT "TWO NUMBERS ARE EQUAL"
```

The essential part of the solution lies in lines 80, 90, and 100. Each time, A(K) will be compared with the values A(K + 1), A(K + 2) and so on. If two numbers are found to be equal, the program jumps to the PRINT statement in line 150. If not, line 130 will be executed and then the program will stop at line 140, thus completing the solution to the problem.

MULTI-DIMENSIONAL ARRAYS

In a DIM statement the name of an array can also be followed by more than one number, separated by commas. Such arrays are called multi-dimensional arrays. If the name is followed by two numbers, it is a two-dimensional array; if there are three numbers, it is a three-dimensional array, and so on.

Here is an example of a two-dimensional array. The instruction:

```
DIM A(3,4)
```

introduces the following variables.

```
A(1,1)   A(1,2)   A(1,3)   A(1,4)
A(2,1)   A(2,2)   A(2,3)   A(2,4)
A(3,1)   A(3,2)   A(3,3)   A(3,4)
```

These variables can be treated in the same way as the variables of a one-dimensional array (like the one previously discussed). For example:

```
10  DIM A(3,4)
20  FOR K=1 TO 3
30  FOR J=1 TO 4
40  LET A(K,J)=10*K+J
50  PRINT A(K,J)
60  NEXT J
70  NEXT K
```

You should now be able to test this program for yourself. The name of an array may in some cases, be the same as the name of an "ordinary" variable. The variables A(1) to A(10) can therefore occur in the same program as the variable A. In order to distinguish between an "ordinary" variable and a variable of an array (sometimes called one of the elements of an array) the latter is referred to as a *subscripted* variable and the former as a *simple* variable.

Chapter 16
Subroutines

The game of chess is no doubt one of the most challenging games for some programmers. Tournaments are held every year. The number of chess-playing computers, or rather the number of chess programs, increases every day.

When you are playing chess, the chess board must be displayed after every move. Fortunately a separate program can be used to display the situation on the board. Each time the board needs to be shown, you can jump from the "main program" to this separate part of the program. When this is finished you can jump back to the main program as if nothing had happened. The separate program to which the program jumps temporarily from the main program is generally referred to as the *subroutine*.

The instruction BASIC uses for jumping to a subroutine is the GOSUB (for go to subroutine) instruction, which always takes the form: GOSUB line number. As a result of this instruction, the program jumps to the specified line number and continues from there. The effect is in fact the same as that of the GOTO instruction. There is, however, a basic difference between the two instructions as the computer, once it has reached the RETURN instruction, returns to the main program and continues with the line following the line containing the GOSUB instruction. The following illustrates this procedure.

```
10   . . .
20   . . .
     . . .
     . . .
100  GOSUB 300                          Main program
110  . . .
     . . .
     . . .
200  GOSUB 300
210  . . .
     . . .
     . . .
270  STOP
300  REM SUBROUTINE STARTS HERE
     . . .                              Subroutine
     . . .
350  RETURN
```

In the example, lines 10 to 270 form the main program. Line 100 calls the subroutine for the first time. The computer continues the program starting with line 300. When it has reached line 350, the computer returns to the main program and continues with line 110. When it has reached line 200 it jumps to line 300 again. When line 350 has been reached the program jumps back again, this time to line 210.

Notice the STOP instruction in line 270. This prevents the computer from once more executing the instructions contained in the subroutine. If this were the case, error report 7 would appear as a result of line 350, as a RETURN is found without a corresponding GOSUB instruction.

The following program may seem unusual, but it gives a clear illustration of the use of the GOSUB instruction. You can provide your own text—The Ballad of the ZX81' perhaps!

```
10  REM SONG TO BE WRITTEN BY THE USER
20  PRINT "  }
30  PRINT "  }    First verse
40  PRINT "  }    (to be filled in by user)
50  GOSUB 150
```

```
 6Ø  PRINT "  }
 7Ø  PRINT "  }  Second verse
 8Ø  PRINT "  }  (to be filled in by user)
 9Ø  GOSUB 15Ø
1ØØ  PRINT "  }
11Ø  PRINT "  }  Third verse
12Ø  PRINT "  }  (to be filled in by user)
13Ø  GOSUB 15Ø
14Ø  STOP
15Ø  REM CHORUS
16Ø  PRINT "  }
17Ø  PRINT "  }  Chorus
18Ø  PRINT "  }  (to be filled in by user)
19Ø  RETURN
```

Finally, it is possible to jump from one subroutine to another subroutine. When the program reaches RETURN, it will jump back to the subroutine from which the second subroutine was called. When the program reaches RETURN again, it jumps back to the main program. If you place the main program and the subroutines side by side, you see the following pattern given in Fig. 16-1.

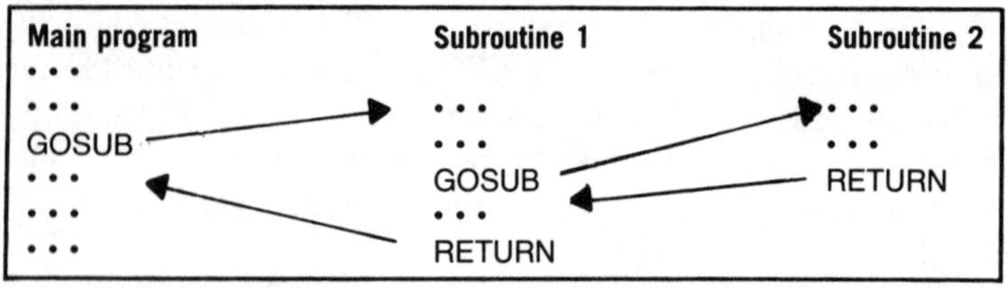

Fig. 16-1. If you place the main program and subroutines side by side, you can see the pattern in which the program lines are executed.

In this way you can string a large number of subroutines together. The situation becomes very interesting when you make a subroutine call itself. This results in recursive subroutines, a subject best left to the experts!

Chapter 17

About Letters and Other Characters

No one can really imagine what life would be without letters. No books, no newspapers, no magazines, no ZX81 manual! It is not surprising, therefore, that computers, too, are good at manipulating letters and characters in general. Word processing is now one of the major fields of application in the computer world, and you can carry out all sorts of word-manipulating operations on the ZX81.

First of all, variables do not only represent numbers. It is possible to assign series of letters to variables as "values." A series of characters is called a *string variable*. In order to distinguish between the variables discussed in previous chapters, numeric variables, and the string variables, which are the subject of this chapter, string variables are always a single letter followed by a dollar sign.

> REMEMBER:
> A name of a string variable must consist of a single letter followed by the dollar sign: $.

Examples of correctly spelled names for string variables are: A$, C$, Z$, and P$. Although most versions of BASIC allow more freedom in naming string variables, ZX81 BASIC restrictions do not result in names that are in conflict with the rules of standard BASIC.

The following program demonstrates that string variables are "real" variables to which various strings of characters can be assigned.

```
10 LET A$="MR"
20 LET B$="SANDMAN"
30 LET C$=A$+B$
40 PRINT "THE NAME IS";C$
50 LET A$="GOOD NIGHT"
60 PRINT A$
```

The result of this program is:

```
THE NAME IS MR SANDMAN
GOOD NIGHT
```

In line 10 the value MR is assigned to the string variable A$. Note that the string is enclosed in the familiar quotation marks. These quotes may not be omitted. As usual, the values are assigned to the variables by means of the keyword LET. In line 20 the string SANDMAN is assigned to B$. The next line shows that we really can manipulate with such strings. Here the string A$+B$ is assigned to the variable C$.

The + sign here means: chain the two strings together. This is called *concatenation*, or *chaining together*. The PRINT instruction in the next line contains two items to be printed. Each of these is a string, but the first string has been included directly in the PRINT statement in the familiar manner, whereas the second string is represented by a string variable. Then the old value of A$ is overwritten by a new value, the string GOOD NIGHT. The plus sign is the only operational sign that we are allowed to use with strings, but this does not mean that only a limited number of manipulations can be carried out with strings. On the contrary, there are a number of powerful functions that can be applied.

The length of the string that may be assigned to a string variable is unlimited, apart from the obvious limitations imposed by the available memory. Table 17-1 lists a number of typical strings.

Various functions can be applied to strings, and you can try a brief example program for each one.

Table 17-1. Some Typical Strings.

String	Comments
"AB"	String consisting of 2 letters.
"AB "	STring consisting of 2 letters and one space. Note that the space is also treated as a character.
" "	String consisting of three spaces.
"1254"	String consisting of 4 characters. The figures here represent a string and not the number 1254. You will see later that there are ways of converting string into numbers.
""	This is a string that does not contain any characters. This very peculiar string can be compared with the number 0.
""""""	String consisting of two quotation marks. Notice that the quotes on the outside mark the beginning and end of the string, so that the actual string contains only the two quotes shown. The quotes on the inside must by typed in using the Q key.

THE LEN FUNCTION

The LEN (length) function gives the number of characters in a string. For instance:

```
LEN "ZX81"
```

gives the number 4, as the string ZX81 consists of 4 characters. Try this example program.

```
1Ø  PRINT "INPUT A NAME"
2Ø  INPUT A$
3Ø  LET LENGTH=LEN A$
4Ø  PRINT "THIS NAME IS ";
5Ø  PRINT LENGTH;
6Ø  PRINT " CHARACTERS LONG"
```

In line 20 there is an INPUT instruction, so you need to input a string. After the RUN command, the text INPUT A NAME will be printed first, followed by quotation marks to remind you that you must now input a string, so type in a name, without the familiar quotation marks. For example:

JANETTE

The computer will then display:

THIS NAME IS 7 CHARACTERS LONG

THE VAL INSTRUCTION

When a string represents a number, it can be converted to that number with the aid of the VAL (value) function, for example:

```
10  LET A$= "2468"
20  LET B$= "WHO DO WE APPRECIATE"
30  LET C=VAL A$
40  LET D=2469-C
50  PRINT D;B$
```

The result of this program will be:

1 WHO DO WE APPRECIATE

In line 10 the string 2468 (not the number 2468) is assigned to the string variable A$. Line 20 speaks for itself. In line 30 the VAL function is applied with the result that the value 2468 is assigned to the numeric variable C (as the name C is not followed by a $ sign). In the following line this value is subtracted from the number 2469. The PRINT instruction finally shows the result.

The VAL function can also be applied to an expression. For example:

```
PRINT VAL "2+SQR(9)"
```

immediately gives the value 5. When the VAL function itself is used in an expression, it must always be the first item. The statement:

```
10  LET A=3+VAL "7"
```

is therefore not correct as VAL "7" is not the first item. The expression should have been:

```
10  LET A=VAL "7" +3
```

The argument of a string function can itself contain a string function. Try out this statement:

```
PRINT VAL (STR$ LEN "TWO")
```

With instructions indicating where something is to be placed on the screen, such as PRINT AT... and the PLOT and UNPLOT functions (discussed in Chapter 18), the VAL function can only be used directly to give the first coordinate. Thus PRINT AT VAL "3",4 is correct, but PRINT AT 3, VAL"4" is not, as the VAL function in the second statement is used to give the second coordinate. Note that the two values following the word AT are called the coordinates, see also Chapter 10. To avoid mistakes, it is wise not to use the VAL function at all in such PRINT statements.

THE STR$ FUNCTION

The STR$ (string) function is in fact the opposite of the VAL function: it converts a number into a string. For example:

```
10  LET A=2468
20  LET P$=" WHO DO WE APPRECIATE"
30  LET K$=STR$ A
40  LET M$=K$+P$
50  PRINT M$
```

The result of this program is:

```
2468 WHO DO WE APPRECIATE
```

In line 30 the string "2468" is assigned to string variable K$ by applying the string function STR$ to the variable A. Apart from this, the program speaks for itself. The argument of the STR$ function can itself be an expression. The string resulting from such an STR$ function is the string that would appear if that expression were displayed by a PRINT statement.

The STR$ function can be particularly useful, for example, if you want to print a list of numbers in such a way that the decimal points are placed exactly beneath each other. Before being printed, each number is assigned to a string variable by means of a STR$ function. After this you can, with the aid of the slicing technique to be discussed shortly, lift the characters one by one out of the string in order to check the position of the decimal point and how many characters are placed before it. On the basis of this information, you can then print the number in exactly the right position using the TAB function.

THE CHR$ AND CODE FUNCTIONS

To understand the next two functions, you need to know that each character corresponds to a certain code number. This applies to all symbols that can be used individually. In Appendix F you will find a complete list. If you refer to this you will see, for example, that the letter A corresponds to code number 38, and vice versa. To see all the symbols displayed on the screen, try this program:

```
10 FOR K=0 TO 255
20 PRINT CHR$ K;
30 NEXT K
```

The ZX81 codes are unique. They are completely different from the often-used ASCII codes, for example. The CHR$ (character) function converts a code into a symbol or character and that a symbol is converted into a code by the CODE function.

The CHR$ function converts a given code number into its corresponding character. You can use the preceding program as an example. In this program the numbers 0 to 255 are assigned to the CHR$ function in succession, and you can use the PRINT instruction to see which symbol each individual number corresponds. The CHR$ function is helpful if you want to print a special symbol that cannot be typed in directly. By using the CHR$ function, you can print the required symbol. You can also apply the CHR$ function if a symbol that is not dependent on a certain result is to be printed.

The argument of a CODE function must always be a string. CODE then gives the code of the first character in the string. For example:

```
10 INPUT A$
20 LET K=CODE A$
30 PRINT K
```

If you input the string "APE", the number 38 will be displayed, as this is the code for A, the first letter of the string. You can use code numbers to arrange words in alphabetical order.

SLICING: THE WORD TO

You may sometimes need to lift a number of characters from a given string. The series of characters that can be "sliced" from the string BASIC is shown in Table 17-2.

Table 17-2. Slicing the String BASIC.

B	A	S	I	C
BA	AS	SI	IC	
BAS	ASI	SIC		
BASI	ASIC			

These strings are called the *substrings* of the original string "BASIC". There is in fact no reason why the empty string " " and the complete string "BASIC" should not be called substrings. On the ZX81, substrings are obtained by means of the slicing technique. In this respect ZX81 BASIC differs from other versions of BASIC. In slicing, the substring is always specified by an expression in parenthesis immediately following the string. The expression generally takes the form: string (start TO finish). For example:

```
"COMPUTER"(2 TO 4)
```

gives the string

```
"OMP"
```

Table 17-3 gives a few more examples.
There is an example program using TO.

```
10 LET A$="COMPUTER"
20 LET NUMBER=LEN A$
30 FOR K=1 TO NUMBER
40 LET B$=A$(1 TO K)
50 PRINT B$
60 NEXT K
```

The result of this program is:

```
C
CO
COM
COMP
```

Table 17-3. Sample Strings.

Expression	Result	Remarks
"COMPUTER" (1 TO 4)	"COMP"	The first 4 letters.
"COMPUTER" (TO4)	"COMP"	If the start is omitted, then 1 is assumed.
"COMPUTER" (6 TO 8)	"TER"	The last 3 letters.
"COMPUTER" (6 TO)	"TER"	If the finish is omitted, then the length of the string is assumed.
"COMPUTER" (1 TO 8)	"COMPUTER"	Substring consists of all the letters, i.e., the entire string.
"COMPUTER" (TO)	"COMPUTER"	If start and finish are omitted the result is the entire string.
"COMPUTER" (10 TO 11)	""	The string contains only 8 characters: the result is the empty string.
"COMPUTER" (4)	"P"	In this way only the forth letter is sliced from the string.

```
COMPU
COMPUT
COMPUTE
COMPUTER
```

Note that in line 20 the LEN instruction assigns the number of characters contained in the string "COMPUTER" to NUMBER. This value is applied in the slicing in line 40. As line 40 is part of a FOR...NEXT loop, the preceding substring is displayed.

By using a LET instruction, you can also assign a series of characters to a substring. Here is an example.

```
10  PRINT "GUESSING GAME"
20  INPUT A$
30  LET LENGTH=LEN A$
40  LET B$=A$
50  LET B$(2 TO LENGTH-1)="**********"
```

```
 60  CLS
 70  PRINT B$
 80  PRINT "WHAT WORD IS THIS?"
 90  INPUT W$
100  IF W$=A$ THEN GOTO 140
110  PRINT "WRONG . . . . THE WORD WAS"
120  PRINT A$
130  STOP
140  PRINT "CORRECT"
```

This game should be played by two people. The first person inputs a name, and the second person sees only the first and last letters. On the basis of this information he must try to guess the word. In line 20, the word that was input is assigned to the string variable A$. In the following line the LEN instruction gives the number of characters. The string is then assigned to B$.

In line 50, you mutilate the contents of the string variable by replacing the second to the penultimate letters by asterisks. The string of asterisks, to the right of the = sign, contains 10 characters. If this number is too large or too small for the given length (2 TO LENGTH–1), some characters will automatically be cut off, starting from the right hand side. If there are two few symbols, spaces will automatically be added, also from the right. This is called *Procrustean assignment*. Procrustes was an inn-keeper who used to make sure that his guests fitted the bed exactly by either stretching them or by cutting of their feet!

In line 60 the screen is cleared by applying the CLS instruction. The part of the game described in lines 70 to 140 does not need any further explanation.

ARRAYS WITH STRINGS

In Chapter 15 the concept of arrays, both ordinary and multidimensional, was examined. Remember that the statement:

```
DIM A(2,3)
```

reserves spaces for the following variables:

```
A(1,1)  A(1,2)  A(1,3)
A(2,1)  A(2,2)  A(2,3)
```

These variables can be treated as all other variables, for example:

```
LET B=A(2,1)+4
```

On the ZX81 arrays with strings can also be used. These are always multi-dimensional arrays and each variable of these arrays can only contain a single character. The name of the array must again be followed by the familiar $ sign. An example of a DIM instruction with a string array is:

```
DIM A$(2,3)
```

A row of string array variables (variables that have the same number before the comma), such as:

```
A$(1,1)   A$(1,2)   A$(1,3)
```

forms one string, and as this string consists of three variables this row can contain a word of three letters. You can refer to a certain row simply by using the number of the row, so:

```
LET A$(1)="BAS"
```

has the result that the letters B, A, and S respectively are assigned to the row A$(1,1), A$(1,2) and A$(1,3). This is illustrated by the following example.

```
10  DIM X$(3,4)
20  FOR K=1 TO 3
30  INPUT X$(K)
40  NEXT K
50  FOR K=3 TO STEP–1
60  PRINT X$(K)
70  NEXT K
```

If you type in succession:

```
DOG
PUSS
MOUSE
```

the computer will give the answer:

```
MOUSE
PUSS
DOG
```

The slicing technique discussed previously can also be used here, for example:

```
LET B$=X$(2)(3 TO 4)
```

If the string “PUSS” was assignd to X$(2), B$ will be “SS”.

Chapter 18
About Pictures

One thing that distinguishes a computer from a calculator is the fact that you can use a computer to "draw" all kinds of pictures on the screen. This facility has a large number of practical uses, including the graphic representation of results, and the creation of visual aids for teachers. With a large number of games, too, pictures are indispensable. You only have to pass an amusement arcade to know that! None of these pictures would be possible without today's computers.

The ZX81 also provides the opportunity to display pictures on the screen. It is even possible to have moving pictures. In the ZX81 brochures, the display of pictures is referred to as *graphics*, and the display of moving shapes is referred to as *animated graphics*. The ZX81 is provided with a separate function, the INKEY$ function, which enables you to react immediately to certain situations on the screen, for example, when playing games.

When working with pictures, the following instructions are important:

1. PRINT AT prints characters and graphic symbols anywhere on the screen.

2. PLOT draws pictures. The screen shows a small black square at a given position. These squares, or picture elements, are known as *pixels*. By placing a large number of these squares side by side, you can draw lines or other shapes.

3. UNPLOT wipes out a black square that has already been displayed. By combining it with PLOT, you can even create moving pictures by plotting one pixel then another one next to it while blanking out the first. This will create a moving square.

4. PAUSE stops the program for a specified length of time.

5. INKEY$ reads the keyboard. This is especially interesting if you want to react immediately to certain situations on the screen.

6. SLOW puts the computer into compute and display mode, in which computing is done relatively slowly. (This does not work on the ZX80 with the upgraded version of BASIC.)

7. FAST puts the computer into the fast mode. In this mode the screen goes blank during computing as the calculations occur too fast to display intermediate stages.

THE PRINT AT INSTRUCTION

The PRINT AT instruction was dealt with in Chapter 10. It always takes the form: PRINT AT line number, position on line, "text." For example:

```
PRINT AT 15, 7;"+"
```

As a result of this instruction the + symbol is displayed on the screen, on the 15 and 7 coordinates. Figure 18-1 shows how the PRINT instruction finds the required position on the screen.

The PRINT AT instruction can reach all positions with an X coordinate of 0 to 31 and a Y coordinate of 0 to 21. Positions that have already been used can be overwritten. Below this area two additional lines are available for displaying text on the screen.

The graphics symbols are particularly interesting when you want to display pictures on the screen. These symbols can only be

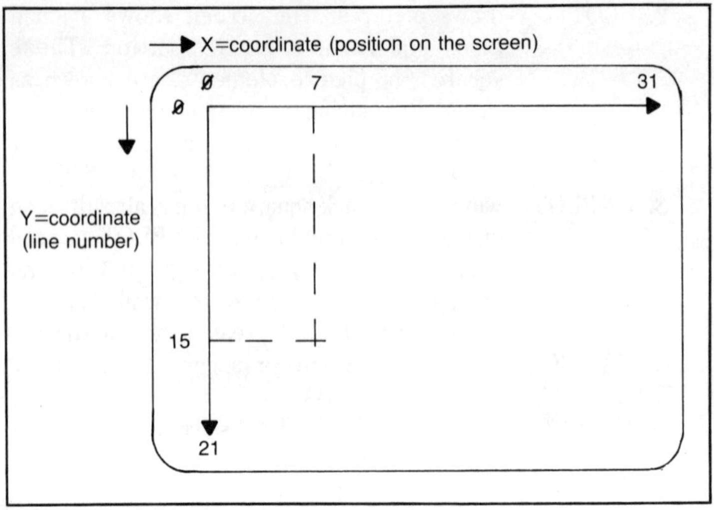

Fig. 18-1. Finding the screen position.

displayed at a specified place by using the PRINT AT instruction. By using the PLOT instruction (discussed shortly), you can only display small black squares. The graphics symbols with corresponding codes are given in Fig. 18-2.

These symbols are also found on the keyboard. For example the graphics symbol "square with chessboard pattern" is on the A key. A graphics symbol is typed in the following way.

1. Press the GRAPHICS key (shifted 9).
2. The G cursor (for graphics) appears on the screen.
3. Press SHIFT, followed by one of the keys that have graphics symbols written on them (for example, the A key if you want to see the chessboard pattern).
4. Continue typing more graphics symbols, until GRAPHICS or NEW LINE is pressed again.
5. The only exception to the above is the space sign (code 0), which can be typed in directly by pressing SPACE.

Alternatively, you can enter each symbol indirectly by using its corresponding code. This is shown in the following program.

```
10  FOR K=128 to 138
20  LET A$=CHR$ K
30  PRINT A$;
40  NEXT K
```

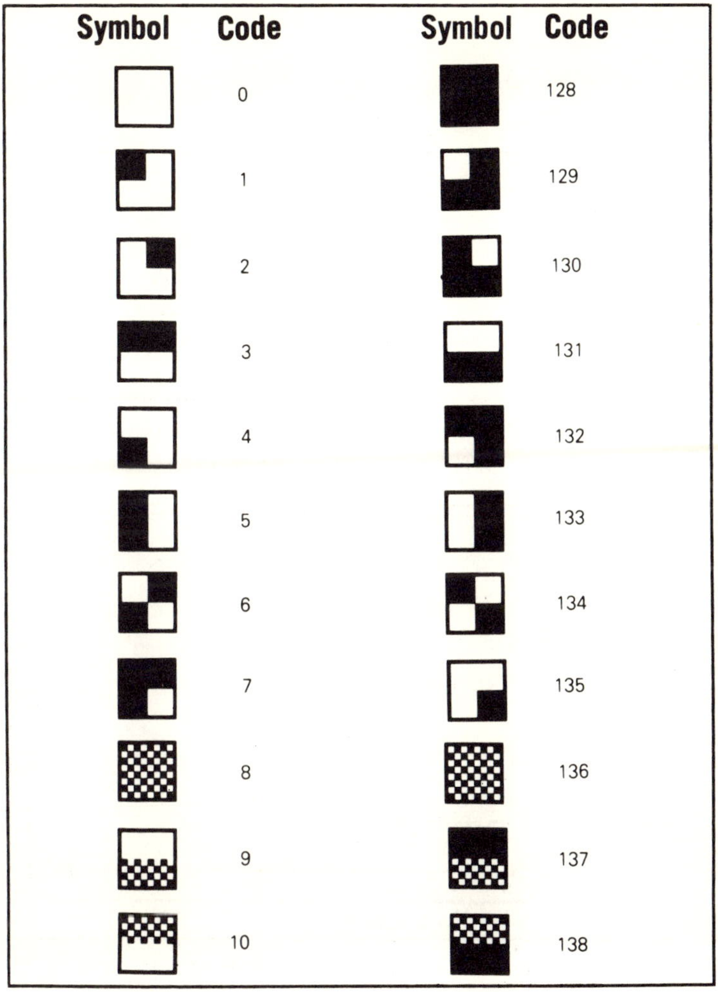

Fig. 18-2. Graphic symbols and their codes.

This results in a bar consisting of the symbols that have the codes 128 to 138.

If a key is pressed while the G (for graphics) cursor is showing, the symbol in question will be shown in white on a black background.

THE PLOT INSTRUCTION

The PLOT instruction always looks like this: PLOT X coordinate, Y coordinate for example:

PLOT 15,7

As a result of this a black square will appear on the screen on the 15 and 7 coordinates. Be careful, though!

> WARNING:
> The coordinates for the PLOT and UNPLOT instructions are different from those for the PRINT AT instruction. When you use PRINT AT, the screen is divided into 32 × 22 character positions. With PLOT and UNPLOT, the screen is divided into 64 × 44 positions. In addition, the 0 coordinate of the Y axis is in a different position.

With a PLOT instruction the X coordinate runs from 0 to 63 and the Y coordinate runs from 0 to 43 as shown in Fig. 18-3.

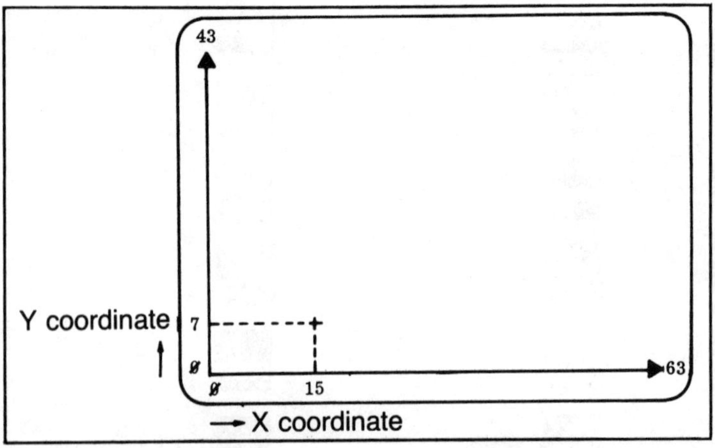

Fig. 18-3. The screen coordinates when the PLOT instruction is used.

Note that the 0 point of the Y coordinate is at the bottom of the screen, whereas with the PRINT AT instruction it is at the top.

The following program enables you to experiment with the two instructions:

```
10 PRINT "X COORD. V. PLOT"
20 INPUT XPLOT
30 PRINT "COORD. V. PLOT
40 INPUT XPLOT
50 PRINT "X COORD. V. PRINT AT"
60 INPUT XPRINT
```

```
70  PRINT "Y COORD. V. PRINT AT"
80  INPUT YPRINT
90  PRINT AT XPRINT,YPRINT;"0"
100 PLOT XPLOT,YPLOT
```

By using the PLOT instruction, you can draw straight lines without any difficulty. The following program shows how a horizontal line with a constant Y coordinate, can be displayed on the screen.

```
10  PRINT "INPUT Y COORDINATE"
20  INPUT Y
30  FOR K=1 TO 63
40  PLOT K,Y
50  NEXT K
```

The key to this program is line 40. As a result of PLOT K,Y a series of adjoining squares with a constant Y coordinate are displayed; therefore, we see a horizontal line at the level of the input Y coordinate. A similar program produces a vertical line.

```
10  PRINT "INPUT X COORDINATE"
20  INPUT X
30  FOR K=1 TO 43
40  PLOT X,K
50  NEXT K
```

You can print a diagonal line by changing both the X coordinate and the Y coordinate in fixed steps in a FOR...NEXT instruction. For instance:

```
10  PRINT "INPUT INCLINATION"
20  INPUT M
30  FOR K=1 TO 63
40  LET XCOR=K
50  LET YCOR=M*XCOR
60  IF YCOR > 43 THE GOTO 80
70  PLOT XCOR,YCOR
80  NEXT K
```

Try out the program for the value M = 1. Note that as a result of line 40, the X coordinate is changed each time in steps of 1 and the V coordinate in steps of M*XCOR, in other words, in steps M times larger than the steps of the X coordinate. The Y coordinate must not exceed 43, as this is the edge of the screen, and line 60 has been included to ensure that it stays within this limit.

In this case the line goes through the 0,0 point (see Fig. 18-3). This point is called the *origin*. It is also possible to raise the line so that it no longer runs through the origin. This is done by altering line 50 as follows:

```
50  LET YCOR=M*COR+B
```

B must already have been given a constant value by using an INPUT instruction. Try this program out for yourself.

You can also plot all kinds of lines and curves. This example is taken from the ZX81 manual.

```
10  FOR N= 0 TO 63
20  PLOT N,22+20*SIN(N/32*3.14)
30  NEXT N
```

This results in the display of a sine wave on the screen. It is interesting to compare this program with the last program in Chapter 14.

THE PAUSE INSTRUCTION

The PAUSE instruction is used to interrupt the computing temporarily. PAUSE is always followed by a number indicating the length of time the program needs to wait. To give you some idea, the number 50 stops the program for about 1 second. For example, this program can turn your computer into a digital clock.

```
 10  FOR H=0 TO 23
 20  FOR M=0 TO 59
 30  FOR S=0 TO 59
 40  PRINT H;" HOUR ";M;" MINUTES"
 50  PRINT "AND ";S;" SECONDS"
 60  PAUSE 50
 65  POKE 16437,255                    (Only for ZX80)
 70  CLS
 80  NEXT S
 90  NEXT M
100  NEXT H
```

This program consists of three FOR...NEXT instructions. The outer loop counts the hours. Inside this there is a loop for counting the minutes and finally a loop for counting the seconds. The innermost loop (lines 30 to 80) contains the necessary PRINT instructions and also the PAUSE instruction.

On the ZX80 with the upgraded version of BASIC (8K ROM) a PAUSE instruction must always be followed by the POKE instruction. For example, in the preceding program the POKE instruction was inserted between lines 60 and 70.

```
65  POKE 16437,255
```

THE INKEY$ INSTRUCTION

When the INKEY$ instruction is entered, it gives an immediate reading of the keyboard. INKEY$ should in fact be regarded as a string variable that can contain one character. As soon as a program executes a line including INKEY$, it reads the keyboard and the key pressed at that moment is then assigned to the variable INKEY$. This value can from then on be treated as an ordinary string consisting of one character. If no key is being pressed at the time when INKEY$ occurs in the program, the result will be the empty string "". The following program illustrates this:

```
1Ø  PRINT INKEY$;
2Ø  GOTO1Ø
```

Note that if you have a ZX80 with upgraded version of BASIC, you need to add 15 PAUSE 50 and 17 POKE 16437, 255.

When this program is run the screen will display the key being pressed at the time. Line 10 indicates that the key you press, which is therefore being assigned to the variable INKEY$, must be printed. If you do not press any key, the empty string "" will be shown, with the result that nothing changes on the screen.

The following program illustrates INKEY$ in an IF instruction:

```
1Ø  PRINT "*";
2Ø  IF INKEY$="S" THEN STOP
3Ø  GOTO 1Ø
```

As a result of this program the screen will be filled with asterisks until you press the S key. As a result of the instruction in line 20, the computer will then stop executing the program.

THE SLOW AND FAST MODES

By using the SLOW and FAST keys you can put the computer in the slow and fast modes. The fast mode runs about 4 times as fast as the slow mode.

When the computer runs in the fast mode, the screen goes blank during computing, and when a program is being typed in, the screen blinks each time a key is pressed. The screen will display a continuous picture only if the end of the program has been reached or if the computer comes across a PAUSE instruction.

When the computer is running in the slow mode the loss of speed is compensated by for by the convenience of a continuous display. This is not possible on the ZX80 with the upgraded version off BASIC. When the ZX81 is switched on it automatically runs in the SLOW mode. It will be clear that the fast mode is preferable if the program involves a lot of computing. For games the slow mode is generally more suitable.

ANIMATED DISPLAYS

Nothing is more amusing than animated displays . . . living pictures. The principle of animated graphics is the same as that of motion pictures. When large numbers of pictures are shown in rapid succession, they give the impression of a moving picture if the individual pictures shift to a slightly different position each time. This means that we can display moving pictures in four ways.

1. By printing a picture on the screen.
2. By displaying a picture for a brief time.
3. By deleting it.
4. By showing it again, but this time in a slightly different position.

The CLS and UNPLOT instructions can be used to blank out the picture. The following program shows a simple example. The ■ is entered by first pressing GRAPHICS, then SPACE, then GRAPHICS again to type in ".

```
10 INPUT SPEED
20 FOR K=0 TO 31
30 PRINT AT 10,K;"■"
40 PAUSE SPEED
45 POKE 16437,255                (Only for the ZX80)
50 CLS
60 NEXT K
```

Line 10 contains an INPUT instruction, which means that you need to input a value to be assigned to SPEED. This is followed by a FOR...NEXT instruction. While this runs, the black square is printed (line 30), shown for a while (lines 40 and 50), and erased again (line 50). Note that the K coordinate is increasing all the time so you get the impression that the black square is moving across the screen.

In the following program a series of black squares is printed in such a way that they form the shape of an airplane. The X coordinate of all these PRINT instructions is also raised continually in a FOR...NEXT instruction. This will give the impression that the plane is flying across the screen. The intention of this game is to shoot down the plane by pressing one of the keys with the numbers 1 to 8. The value 1 corresponds to the position on the far left and 8 to the position on the far right. Ten airplanes in all will fly across the screen. The program is designed in such a way that you can only fire once at each plane. If you hit a plane, the screen displays:

```
HIT
```

The program has to be economical of text so that it can squeeze into the 1K memory. When the RUN command is given the question:

```
V=
```

will appear on the screen. You must enter a number giving the speed of the plane. At the end of the game the number of hits is displayed.

Finally a tip with regard to typing in the program. You get the black squares by putting the computer in the GRAPHICS mode and then pressing SPACE. If you want to type in an ordinary space (represented here by b), you must first press GRAPHICS, which puts the computer in a different mode again. After this, spaces will be white squares again.

PROGRAM FOR SHOOT DOWN THE PLANE.

```
 2 PRINT "V="
 4 INPUT SN
 5 LET A=Ø
 6 RAND
 8 FOR K=1 TO 1Ø
1Ø CLS
```

```
12  LET VL=Ø
14  LET W$=""
16  LET R=INT((RND*15)+1.)
18  FOR X=Ø TO 24
2Ø  GOSUB 60
22  PAUSE SP
24  POKE 16437,255                    (Only for the ZX80)
26  CLS
28  IF INKEY="" THEN GOTO 48
3Ø  IF VL=1 THEN GOTO 48
32  LET W$=INKEY$
34  LET VL=1
38  LET U=3*VAL W$
4Ø  IF ABS (X-U)>2 THEN GOTO 48
42  PRINT AT Ø,Ø;"HIT"
43  LET A=A+1
44  PAUSE 1ØØ
45  POKE 16437,255                    (Only for the ZX80)
46  GOTO 5Ø
48  NEXT X
5Ø  NEXT X
52  PRINT A
54  STOP
6Ø  PRINT AT R,X;"bb ■"
62  PRINT AT R+1,X;"■ bb ■■"
64  PRINT AT R+2,X;"■ ■ ■ ■ ■ ■"
66  PRINT AT R+3,X;"bbb ■ ■"
68  PRINT AT R+4,X;"bb ■"
7Ø  RETURN
```

ZX81 owners can find out what happens if line 22, containing the PAUSE instruction, is omitted.

The program which draws a horizontal line (see Chapter 17) shows the best possibilities for displaying moving objects with the aid of BASIC instructions. Try running this program again, this time making each loop delete the point shown last. The combination PLOT and UNPLOT can lead to some very attractive results. However, the best moving pictures are achieved by using machine code instructions.

Chapter 19
Using a Cassette Recorder and a Printer

Machines that can be connected to a computer are usually referred to as *peripheral devices*, two of which a cassette recorder and a printer, will be discussed in this chapter.

A cassette recorder is used for storing a program on tape. This obviates the need to type in the program every time you want to run it. All you need to do is to "load" the program from the cassette recorder. The cassette recorder can also be used for playing preprogrammed cassette tapes.

A printer is used for printing text and program listings on paper.

CASSETTE RECORDERS

The ZX81 is supplied with leads that connect it to an ordinary mono cassette recorder, preferably one with a counter that uses low-noise tapes.

Saving a program on tape from the memory is done as follows.

1. Connect the leads: connect the EAR socket on the computer to the EAR socket on the cassette recorder. Connect

the MIC socket on the computer with the MIC socket on the cassette recorder. If the leads are accidentally crossed over, no damage will be done to the ZX81.

2. Position the tape in a blank section ready to record. If you wish, you can first speak the name of the program into the microphone. This makes it easier to find the program afterwards.
3. If, for instance, you want the following short program, which is stored in the memory, to be recorded on tape, you give the SAVE command, followed by a name of your choice.

```
10 REM THIS IS THE ONLY LINE
```

Then press NEW LINE. On no account press NEW LINE immediately after giving this SAVE command.

4. Start the tape recorder, usually by pressing RECORD and PLAY.
5. Press NEW LINE.
6. The screen will be a grayish color, then you see various stripes and sometimes hear the most horrific noises! This is quite normal, and after a while the report 0/0 should appear on the screen.
7. The only way to check that the recording has been successful is to load the program back into the computer.

Loading a program from cassette tape to memory is done as follows.

1. Make sure that the EAR socket is connected to the earphone socket on the tape recorder. Sometimes the external loudspeaker socket of the cassette recorder is used as this occasionally produces a stronger signal.
2. Position the tape in the required position and turn the volume control to about ¾ of the maximum volume. If the recorder has tone controls then adjust these to high tones.
3. Type in: LOAD name of the program. For example:

```
LOAD LINE
```

Do not press NEW LINE yet. It is possible to omit the name. The computer then loads the first program it comes across.

4. Play the tape (press PLAY) and then press NEW LINE. Again you will see strange pictures and sometimes hear awful noises. With some tape recorders it is possible to turn down the sound, which is probably advisable if you want to preserve peace in the home.
5. After a while the report 0/0 should appear. If this does not happen you can interrupt the loading action by pressing BREAK. You then repeat the procedure and try to adjust the controls. When you finally get a satisfactory result, make a note of the position of the controls.

Here are a few useful tips to remember when using a tape recorder. It may take a few attempts before you are successful, so keep trying.

1. Sometimes you need to use the loudspeaker socket of the tape recorder.
2. Try cleaning the tape heads in the cassette recorder using the special cleaning tapes available.
3. When you listen to the tape, the silent parts should not make a buzzing noise.
4. The EAR lead may sometimes need to be disconnected when saving programs on tape.

THE PRINTER

Sinclair supplies a separate printer for the ZX81 and there are two instructions/commands for this device.

LLIST is similar to LIST, but all the text is printed on paper.

LPRINT works in the same way as PRINT, but use the printer instead of the television screen.

The COPY instruction prints out a copy of what appears on the television screen.

Chapter 20
Machine Code

The main purpose of this book is to explain how various kind of operations can be carried out on the ZX81 with the aid of the BASIC programming language. In most cases the ZX81 will be used exclusively as a BASIC computer. Programming by means of machine code is much more complex and is often very difficult for a beginner, so it will not be discussed in great detail in this book. Those who are particularly interested in this subject should refer to a specialist book on the subject.

This chapter will be confined to three areas.

1. Explaining the main principles of programming in machine code.
2. Discussing when it is necessary to use machine code.
3. Dealing with the PEEK, POKE, and USR instructions.

WHAT IS MACHINE CODE?

Machine code is the most basic set of instructions that the computer uses. In fact, they are the only instructions the computer can understand. Every program (including all BASIC programs) is ultimately converted into these machine code instructions. This conversion is, of course, carried out by a program in machine code.

Machine code consist of sets of ones and zeros. A more compact notation which is often used is the hexadecimal system, a number system consisting of the symbols 0 to 9 and A to F. By using this system it is possible to represent the various sets of ones and zeros in a simple manner. To express the actions of the machine code instructions more clearly, a language similar to the machine code has been developed. This language is the assembly language. The ZX81 contains a Z80 processor, which means that only assembly languages designed for the Z80 are suitable for use with the ZX81.

WHEN IS MACHINE CODE USED?

Designers of computer systems are often involved with machine code. The ZX81 contains a program built into the ROM memory, which translates BASIC instructions into machine code instructions. This program is written in assembly language.

Generally speaking, machine code is used:

1. If the BASIC language is inadequate for a certain job, for example when the computer is linked to very special equipment.
2. If a program needs to be extremely fast; the fastest way of solving a problem is by using machine code.
3. If you want to make changes in existing programs, for example the existing BASIC program.

These examples illustrate that the main uses of machine code are outside the scope of this book, but BASIC does contain a number of instructions by which the machine code can be called into use.

THE POKE, PEEK, AND USR INSTRUCTIONS

In order to get down to the level of machine code, you need to be able to store series of ones and zeros direct in memory locations. You must also be able to read values from memory locations. You can do these things by using the POKE and PEEK instructions.

With the POKE instruction you can store a given value at a given memory location. It takes the form: POKE memory location, number, for example:

```
POKE 16437,255
```

The number 255 is then converted into a series of ones and zeros according to the binary notation.

The PEEK instruction is used for reading a value from a given memory location. Takes the form: PEEK memory location, for example:

```
LET 1=PEEK 16437
```

The variable 1 will then be given the value which corresponds to the series of ones and zeros found in memory location, or address, 16437. This value will ultimately be assigned as an "ordinary" decimal number.

The USR instruction makes a BASIC program continue with a series of machine-code instructions when it has got to a given address. When the machine-coded instructions have been executed as a subroutine, the BASIC program continues. It takes the form: USR memory location.

From these descriptions you can see that a series of ones and zeros is sometimes converted into a decimal number (PEEK) and a decimal number is sometimes converted into a series of ones and zeros (POKE), both according to the rules of the binary notation. A binary number consists of the digits 0 and 1, the position of a digit being represented by the power of 2. The positions are counted from the right, and you always start counting at 0. For example:

10101101
Zero position
Second position
Third position
Fifth position
Seventh position

This number then represents:

1 in zero position	$1 \times 2^0 = 1$
1 in second position	$1 \times 2^2 = 4$
1 in third position	$1 \times 2^3 = 8$
1 in fifth position	$1 \times 2^5 = 32$
1 in seventh position	$1 \times 2^7 = 128$

Total: $1 + 4 + 8 + 32 + 128 = 173$

A decimal number is converted into a binary number by subtracting powers of 2 from the number, always subtracting the greatest possible power. The following example converts 173 into a series of ones and zeros.

$$
\begin{array}{rcl}
 & & 173 \\
2^7 & = & \underline{128} \quad - \\
 & & 45
\end{array}
$$

(The greatest possible power of 2)

$$
\begin{array}{rcl}
 & & 32 \\
2^5 & = & \underline{} \quad - \\
 & & 13
\end{array}
$$

(Is now the greatest possible power)

$$
\begin{array}{rcl}
2^3 & = & \underline{8} \quad - \\
 & & 5
\end{array}
$$

(Is now the greatest possible power)

$$
\begin{array}{rcl}
2^2 & = & \underline{4} \quad - \\
\end{array}
$$

(Is now the greatest possible power)

$$2^0 = 1$$

(Is a power of 2, or 2^0)

The numbers 2^7, 2^5, 2^3, 2^2, and 2^0 again form the binary number: 1 0 1 0 1 1 0 1, as above.

Appendices

Appendix A
Error Reports

If an obvious error is made during the typing of a line, an S cursor will appear to the right of the error when NEW LINE is pressed. This error must be corrected before the line can be added to the program. Once a program has been typed in, it will be executed when the RUN command is given. The computer will always give a report such as:

```
Ø/6Ø
```

The second number is the number of the last line executed. The first number is the error report code. When a program has been designed correctly, the first number will be 0, as shown. The table on the following pages give the meaning of the other report codes with the situations in which they can occur.

Code	Meaning	Situation in Which This Report Can Occur
Ø	No error found during execution of the program. This report also occurs if the program jumps to a non-existent line number that is bigger than any existing line number.	Any, GOTO, GOSUB
1	The control variable has not been set up by a FOR instruction, but there is an ordinary variable with that name.	NEXT
2	In an expression, a variable is used which has not yet been defined. A subscripted variable is used before space has been reserved for it by means of the DIM instruction (and the initial value 0 has not been assigned). In FOR . . . NEXT statement where the control variable has not been given an initial value, when there is no ordinary variable with the same name.	Any, DIM FOR...NEXT
3	The subscript of a variable in an array is not in accordance with the DIM statement, e.g., DIM A(10) does not allow the use of A(11). If the dimension is negative or bigger than 65535, report B will appear.	Variables of an array, DIM
4	A message which occurs often on a computer which only has a standard memory: "not enough room in memory." As a result of this shortage of space the line number after the / may be incomplete.	LET, INPUT, DIM, PRINT, LIST, PLOT, UNPLOT, FOR, GOSUB, and sometimes during function evaluation
5	There is no more room on the screen for further display. Press CONT; this will clear the screen and the program will be continued.	PRINT, LIST
6	Calculations result in numbers that are too large, the so-called "overflow." Overflow occurs when the result of a calculation is greater than about 10^{38}, e.g., as a result of dividing by 0.	During calculations

Code	Meaning	Situation in Which This Report Can Occur
7	A RETURN instruction is found that has not been preceded by a GOSUB instruction. One of the situations where this report occurs is when the subroutine has not been separated from the main program by a STOP instruction or in another way.	RETURN
8	The user tries to give INPUT as a command. INPUT is the only instruction that cannot be used as a command.	INPUT
9	Result of a STOP instruction. If CONT is pressed next, the program will continue with the line following the STOP instruction (if there is such a line).	STOP
A	The argument of the function is invalid, e.g., a negative number is given as the argument to the SQR function.	SQR, LN, ASN, ACS
B	The Integer is outside the range allowed, e.g., the program jumps to a non-existent address. If an instruction, command, or function requires an integer value and a real value is given, the latter number will automatically be rounded down. If the rounded number is outside the permitted range, error B results. The subscript of an array variable is negative or greater than 65535.	RUN, RAND, POKE DIM, GOTO, GOSUB LIST, LLIST, PAUSE, PLOT, UNPLOT, CHR$, PEEK, USR, AT
C	The string that has to be evaluated as a numerical expression by VAL does not form a valid numerical expression, e.g., PRINT VAL "12A4".	VAL
D	When a program is interrupted by BREAK.	At the end of any instruction or with LOAD, SAVE, LPRINT, LLIST, or COPY
E	The INPUT line starts with STOP.	INPUT
F	When storing the program on cassette tape, no name is given after SAVE.	SAVE

IF THERE ARE ANY PROBLEMS

In practice one may often find that the memory is full especially if your computer only has the standard memory. When this is the case, some very odd things can happen. Text may suddenly disappear or the computer no longer responds to commands. Here are some of the most common situations.

1. During the display of information, report 5 appears. Press CONT, after this the program will continue. You can try this out with the following program:

```
10 FOR K=1 TO 100
20 PRINT K
30 NEXT K
```

   It will often be possible to include CLS instructions in the program to prevent the screen from filling up.
2. During the running of a program report 4 appears. Press CLEAR. Then study the listing and decide where the program can be trimmed (shorter names, shorter line numbers, omit REM statements, and so on).
3. Strange things happen while a program is being typed in. Sometimes you will find that text disappears and the computer no longer responds to commands. Press RUBOUT repeatedly until the cursor reappears and the program responds to commands again. Then look at the listing to work out how you can save space.
4. The program reacts strangely to an INPUT instruction. Press STOP (in the case of a string, first press RUBOUT). Look at the listing to decide how the program can be trimmed, or how memory space can be saved.
5. The program goes on computing. This happens with programs such as:

```
10 GOTO 20
20 GOTO 10
```

If this happens, you need to give the BREAK command. You can also use this command if during loading from cassette tape, the computer continues with the loading action.

Appendix B
Functions

Below you will find a brief summary of the functions available on the ZX81. Note: functions that result in a string are followed by the $ sign. Mathematical functions operate with numbers that are accurate to 9 or 10 digits, so that the calculated result of the function is usually accurate to 8 digits.

Function	Argument	Result
ABS	Number	Gives the absolute value, e.g., ABS(−1) = 1.
ACS	Number	Calculates the arc cosine in radians. The argument must be between −1 and 1.
AND	Two arguments required, the one on the right must be a number	The expression X < 1 AND Y > 2 is only true if both relations are true. For numbers: $A \text{ AND } B = \begin{cases} A \text{ if } B \neq 0 \\ 0 \text{ if } B = 0 \end{cases}$ For a string: A$ and B = A$ if B ≠ 0 "" if B = 0
ASN	Number	Calculates the arc sine in radians. The argument must be between −1 and 1.

Function	Argument	Result
AT	Two numbers	Gives the X and Y coordinates and so decides where an item will be printed, e.g., in PRINT AT 5,5;"*".
ATN	Number	Calculates the arc tangents in radians.
CHR$	Number	Gives the symbol, corresponding to the code. If the argument is not a whole number, it is first rounded.
CODE	String	Gives the code of the first character of the string. If the string is empty, the result of the function is 0.
COS	Number (in radians)	Calculates the cosine.
EXP	Number	Calculates the value e to the power number.
INKEY$	No argument	Reads the keyboard. The result is the character given by the key pressed (if the cursor shows the L mode).
INT	Number	Always rounds down a number, e.g., INT(3.7) = 3 and INT (−3.7) = −4. INT (A + 0.5) rounds A to the nearest integer.
LEN	String	Gives the number of characters of the string, e.g., LEN "APE" = 3.
LN	Number	Gives the logarithm with the base e. To find the logarithm with base 10, divide by LN(2). The argument must be greater than 0.
NOT	Relation or number	NOT $X < 2$ is true if the expression $X < 2$ is false and vice versa; if $X < 2$ is true the entire expression (with NOT) is false. NOT with a number gives 0 if the argument $\neq 0$, otherwise it gives the value 1.
OR	Two relations or two numbers	The expression $X < 1$ OR $Y > 1$ is false only if both relations are false. For numbers: $A \text{ OR } B = \begin{cases} 1 & \text{if } B \neq 0 \\ A & \text{if } B = 0 \end{cases}$
PEEK	Number	Gives the content of the byte in the memory whose address is given by the argument. If necessary, the argument is rounded first. The argument must be in the range 0 – 65535.
PI	—	Gives the value π, i.e., 3.14159265. The keyboard shows the π symbol (under the M key), but the screen displays PI.
RND	—	Gives a random number. The random numbers are in a fixed sequence. The

Function	Argument	Result
		point where the computer starts the selection of random numbers is decided by giving the "RAND number" instruction. If the number = 0 the length of time the TV has been on decides the place.
SGN	Number	Gives the sign of the number, e.g., SGN(−3) = − 1, SGN(0) = 0, SGN(3) = 1.
SIN	Number (in radians)	Calculates the sine.
SQR	Number	Gives the square root of the number, e.g., SQR(9) = 3. The argument must be greater than or equal to 0.
STR$	Number	Gives the string that would be displayed if the number, or the expression, were part of a PRINT statement, e.g., STR$ gives "3".
TAB	Number	Gives column number in a PRINT statement.
TAN	Number (in radians)	Calculates the tangent.
USR	Number	Calls a machine-code program from within the BASIC program. The starting address of this subroutine is given by the argument of the function. If necessary, the argument is rounded first. The result is the contents of the bc register pair. The argument must be in the range 0 – 65535.
VAL	String	Evaluates the string as if it is a numerical expression, e.g., VAL"3 + 5" = 8. If the VAL function itself is part of an expression it must always be the first item, e.g., LET X = VAL"3 + 5" + 4.

Appendix C
Special Symbols

The following symbols are used in calculations.

Symbol	Meaning
+	Addition. This is the only operator that is also used for strings, and there it is used to chain strings together.
–	Subtraction
*	Multiplication
/	Division
**	Raising to a power (entered by pressing the H key).
( )	Parentheses are used in algebra; used to give priority to certain operations.
=	After the LET instruction, this sign means "becomes": LET N = N + 1 means N becomes the previous value of N + 1.

There is also a series of symbols used with relations. A relation is an expression used in an IF...THEN instruction, for example, IF X < 3 THEN PRINT X. In this statement X < 3 is a relation that is true or false, depending on the momentane value of

X. The < sign shows the relation between X and 3 and is called a *relation*. The following relations may be used. There is a separate key for each of these symbols.

Symbol	Meaning
=	Equals
>	Greater than
> =	Greater than or equal to
<	Less than
< =	Less than or equal to
< >	Not equal to

This table explains the remaining symbols.

Symbol	Meaning
⇦	Move the cursor one place to the left.
⇩	Move the cursor one place down.
⇧	Move the cursor one place up.
⇨	Move the cursor one place to the right.
“ ”	On the Q key; quote image within a string.
$	Always follows the name of a string variable.
“	Quotation marks: always used before and after a string, e.g., PRINT “LAST” and LET $ = “FIRST”.
:	Has no special meaning on the ZX81. With other BASICS it is sometimes used to include text in an INPUT statement, but this is not used on the ZX81.
;	Used with a PRINT instruction to indicate that one item must be printed immediately following the last item.
?	Has no special meaning on the ZX81. With other BASICS it is sometimes used to indicate that something needs to be entered as a result of an INPUT instruction.
,	General symbol used to separate arguments, e.g., in DIM, PLOT, UNPLOT, and POKE statements. In a PRINT statement the symbol is used to separate two items and it makes the computer print the items in two columns.
.	Decimal point in a number, e.g., 3.7. Apart from this it has no special meaning.

Appendix D
Priority

The priority rules say how expressions must be evaluated. Multiplication, for instance, has a higher priority than addition, so in the expression:

```
LET A=3+4*2
```

A will be given the value 3 + (4*2) = 11 and not the value (3 + 4) * 2 = 14.

When there is equal priority, an expression is evaluated from left to right. Thus the expression:

```
LET A=4/2*8
```

gives the value (4/2)*8 = 16 and not 4/(2*8) = 0.25.

The following list gives the various operations and their priority. The priority is represented by a number: the higher the number, the higher the priority. You will see, for instance, that multiplication has a higher priority than addition. These rules can be circumvented by using parentheses.

Operation	Priority Number
Subscribing a variable in an array	12
Slicing	12
All functions (except NOT)	11
Raising to a power: **	10
– sign to negate a number, in an expression where – is not placed between two numbers, e.g., LET A = –2	9
Multiplication and division: * and /	8
Addition and subtraction: + and –	6
=,>,<,<=,>=,<>	5
NOT	4
AND	3
OR	2

Appendix E
Instructions and Commands

Below you will find a summary of the various instructions and commands. With the exception of INPUT, all instructions can also be used as commands. The most interesting instruction in this connection is the PRINT instruction. For instance, as a result of this instruction:

```
PRINT 25*35
```

the screen will immediately display the answer 875. In cases like this we speak of a direct PRINT instruction. Commands can also be included in programs. The ZX81 does not make any distinction between terms that are commonly used as instructions and those generally used as commands. The screen is always cleared before a command is executed except in the case of COPY. The notation here is that used in the official ZX81 manual.

Symbol	Meaning
α	Represents a single letter
v	Represents a variable
x,y,z	Represent numeric expressions
m,n	Represent numeric expressions that are always rounded to the nearest integer

Symbol	Meaning
e	Represents an expression or a string
f	Represents a string value expression
s	Represents an instruction

Here is a list of the various instructions and commands.

Instruction or Command	Meaning
CLEAR	Deletes all assigned values of variables. The memory is cleared in the same way. If you want to trace errors in a program by means of PRINT instructions, it is wise to give the CLEAR command before running the program.
CLS	Clears the screen. The picture displayed on the screen is called the display file. It is part of the memory.
CONT	If the program stops with the report p/q (e.g., 9/40 so p = 9 and q = 40), typing CONT will have the following effect. If p ≠ 9 the program will continue with line number q, otherwise it goes to the following line. CONT is used mainly to continue the program when the screen is full.
COPY	Sends a copy of the display to the printer.
DIM $\alpha(n_1,..,n_k)$	This statement clears a space for $n_1 x n_2 x ... n_k$ variables. These variables can then be called up in the program by using the name α and the subscripts n_1 to n_k. Example: DIM A(10) reserves space for the variables A(1) to A(10). These variables can be used in the same way as all other variables, e.g., LET A(3) = 4 + A(1). The set of variables introduced in this way is called the array. The initial value of each variable is 0. An existing array with the name α is deleted as a result of the DIM statement with the same name. If there is not enough room in the memory, error report 4 appears. In ZX81 BASIC, unlike some other BASICS, variables of an array must always be introduced by a DIM instruction.
DIM $\alpha\$(n_1,..,n_k)$	As above, but this instruction applies to string variables. There is a difference, however, in that the final subscript indicates the fixed length of the string. Thus DIM A$(5.10) in fact introduces 5 string variables, which can contain strings of 10 characters, e.g., LET A$(3) = "A1B4C6D8E0".

Instruction or command	Meaning
FAST	Makes the computer run in the FAST mode. The picture is displayed only at the end of a program, during an INPUT statement and during a PAUSE instruction (only for the ZX81).
FOR α = x TO y Step z (NEXTα)	As a result of this instruction, all instructions between FOR α = x etc., and NRXT α for the values α, $\alpha + z$, $\alpha + 2z$, $\alpha + 3z$ etc., will be executed repeatedly until the computed value is y − z or equal to y. The variable α is called the control variable.
FOR α = x TO y (NEXT α)	As above, but now the control variable is automatically increased by 1 each time. If you run this short program: 1Ø FOR K=1 TO 1Ø 2Ø PRINT K 3Ø NEXT K the screen will display the numbers 1 to 10 successively.
GOSUB n (RETURN)	The program continues with the line number indicated. When the computer comes across the RETURN instruction, the program continues with the line following the GOSUB instruction. The part-program executed as a result of this temporary jump is called the subroutine. Note that n can be a numerical expression instead of a number.
GOTO n	The program continues with line number n, or, if n does not exist, the first line after n. Note that n does not need to be a simple number, but can be a numerical expression. This makes it possible to copy the ON . . . GOTO instruction, which is not allowed on the ZX81.
IF x THEN s	If x is true, then s is executed. If x is false the program goes to the next line. For example, IF x <0 THEN GOTO 100. If x is less than 0 the program continues with line 100.
INPUT v	Instructs the user to type in an expression. In the case of a number, the L cursor appears. If a string is required, quotation marks are shown. This instruction temporarily stops the program. It will not continue until the value of the variable is typed

Instruction or command	Meaning
	in and NEW LINE is pressed, e.g., INPUT A (for a number) and INPUT B$ (for a string). Instead of a number (or a single string) an expression can be typed in. This will then automatically be converted into a number (or a string). The program is interrupted by the STOP instruction. If a string variable is expected STOP must be preceded by RUBOUT.
LET v = e	Instruction that assigns the value of the expression e to the variable v. The = sign here means "becomes." Thus LET A = 3 means: A becomes 3; and LET A = A + 3 means A will have the value A had originally + 3. The word LET must be included. In the case of a string variable of fixed length (in an array, or when slicing) e will be shortened or filled with spaces.
LIST	Displays the program on the screen.
LIST N	Displays the program on the screen, starting at line N. If the program is too long, two error reports can appear. If the memory is full, code 4 appears and if the screen is full but the memory is not yet full, error 5 will appear, in which case use the CONT instruction.
LLIST	As LIST O, but using the printer instead of the television. Normally there should not be any problems if the printer is not attached. If there are any problems, the program can be interrupted by BREAK.
LLIST N	As LIST N but using the printer instead of the television. Normally there should not be any problems if the printer is not attached. If there should be any problems the program can be interrupted by BREAK.
LOAD f	For loading a program called f from cassette tape to memory. If f does not exist, the first program available on the tape is loaded. If something goes wrong, stop the program using BREAK, then clear the memory using NEW, adjust the tape recorder controls, and restart the LOAD action.
LPRINT	As PRINT, but using the printer instead of the television. A line is printed in the following instances. 1. When the program jumps from one line to the next. 2. After a LPRINT instruction that does not end in, or ;.

Instruction or command	Meaning
	3. When a comma or TAB instruction requires a new line. 4. At the end of the program. The line number in an AT item is ignored.
NEW	The memory is cleared so that a new BASIC program can be entered.
NEXT α	See FOR α = x TO STEP z.
PAUSE n	Stops computing and displays the display file for n frames of the television (n = 50 gives a pause of about 1 second). The pause can be interrupted by pressing a key. On the ZX80 this instruction must always be followed by POKE 16437,255.
PLOT m,n	The PLOT function blacks in certain areas. The screen is divided into 0-63 horizontal and 0-43 vertical positions. PLOT m,n will black in the pixel with the coordinated m and n. This also moves the print position to the point indicated.
POKE m,n	Writes the value m to the byte in store with address n. m can have a value between 0 and 65535 and n a value between 0 and 255. Used mainly to include machine-code instructions in the program.
PRINT. . .	General instruction to display something on the screen. ; as the final symbol will print the next item immediately following the last one. , as the final symbol will print the next item in the next column. Items to be printed must always be separated by, and strings must be enclosed in " signs. If the result is too big or too small to be displayed in digits, the computer will automatically start to use scientific notation. PRINT by itself simply causes the program to skip a line. The PRINT position can be controlled by using the following. 1. The TAB function 2. The AT function 3. The PLOT instruction When the screen is full, error report 5 occurs. You can continue the program by using the CONT command.

Instruction or command	Meaning
RAND	As RAND O (see RAND n).
RAND n	Indicates where the selection of random numbers is to start. Always used with RND function.
REM	Used to include comments in a program that will not be displayed during the running of the program. It takes the form: line number REM comments. Each new line of comments must start with a higher line number and REM.
RETURN	Used with a subroutine to return to main program. (See GOSUB)
RUN	As RUN O (see RUN n)
RUN n	Clears all variables and starts to execute the program at the line number given (if n does not exist it starts the next number after n).
SAVE f	Used to record a program stored in the memory on tape. f names the program.
SCROLL	Scrolls the display move up one line, losing the top line and making an empty line available at the bottom.
SLOW	Puts the computer into compute and display mode (slow mode) in which the display file is displayed continuously (only on the ZX81).
STOP	This instruction stops the program (report code 9). CONT will resume the program.
UNPLOT m,n	See PLOT m,n. If a pixel with coordinates m and n is black, UNPLOT will blank it out.

Appendix F
Symbols, Graphics, and Codes

Below you will find a complete list of all symbols and graphics on the ZX81 with their codes. Note that there are a few codes that are not used and therefore do not have any corresponding symbols. The ZX81 operating manual also gives the codes for assembler programming, but these are outside the scope of this book.

The word, *inverse* means that a symbol is shown white on a black background.

Code	Symbol	Code	Symbol	Code	Symbol
0	space	16	(	32	4
1	▘	17	)	33	5
2	▝	18	>	34	6
3	▀	19	<	35	7
4	▖	20	=	36	8
5	▌	21	+	37	9
6	▞	22	–	38	A
7	▛	23	*	39	B
8	▒	24	/	40	C
9	🮏	25	;	41	D
10	🮎	26	,	42	E
11	"	27	.	43	F
12	£	28	0	44	G
13	$	29	1	45	H
14	:	30	2	46	I
15	?	31	3	47	J

Code	Symbol	Code	Symbol	Code	Symbol
48	K	103		158	inverse 2
49	L	104		159	inverse 3
50	M	105		160	inverse 4
51	N	106		161	inverse 5
52	O	107		162	inverse 6
53	P	108		163	inverse 7
54	Q	109		164	inverse 8
55	R	110		165	inverse 9
56	S	111		166	inverse A
57	T	112	cursor ⇧	167	inverse B
58	U	113	cursor ⇩	168	inverse C
59	V	114	cursor ⇦	169	inverse D
60	W	115	cursor ⇨	170	inverse E
61	X	116	GRAPHICS	171	inverse F
62	Y	117	EDIT	172	inverse G
63	Z	118	NEWLINE	173	inverse H
64	RND	119	RUBOUT	174	inverse I
65	INKEY$	120	K or L mode	175	inverse J
66	PI	121	FUNCTION	176	inverse K
67		122		177	inverse L
68		123		178	inverse M
69		124		179	inverse N
70		125		180	inverse O
71		126	number	181	inverse P
72		127	cursor	182	inverse Q
73		128	█	183	inverse R
74		129	▟	184	inverse S
75		130	▙	185	inverse T
76		131	▄	186	inverse U
77		132	▜	187	inverse V
78		133	▐	188	inverse W
79		134	▚	189	inverse X
80		135	▗	190	inverse Y
81		136	▒	191	inverse Z
82		137	▓	192	“ ”
83		138	▓	193	AT
84		139	inverse“	194	TAB
85		140	inverse £	195	not used
86		141	inverse $	196	CODE
87		142	inverse :	197	VAL
88		143	inverse ?	198	LEN
89		144	inverse (	199	SIN
90		145	inverse)	200	COS
91		146	inverse>	201	TAN
92		147	inverse <	202	ASN
93		148	inverse =	203	ACS
94		149	inverse +	204	ATN
95		150	inverse –	205	LN
96		151	inverse *	206	EXP
97		152	inverse /	207	INT
98		153	inverse ;	208	SQR
99		154	inverse ,	209	SGN
100		155	inverse .	210	ABS
101		156	inverse 0	211	PEEK
102		157	inverse 1	212	USR

Code	Symbol
213	STR$
214	CHR$
215	NOT
216	**
217	OR
218	AND
219	< =
220	> =
221	< >
222	THEN
223	TO
224	STEP
225	LPRINT
226	LLIST
227	STOP
228	SLOW
229	FAST
230	NEW
231	SCROLL
232	CONT
233	DIM
234	REM
235	FOR
236	GOTO
237	GOSUB
238	INPUT
239	LOAD
240	LIST
241	LET
242	PAUSE
243	NEXT
244	POKE
245	PRINT
246	PLOT
247	RUN
248	SAVE
249	RAND
250	IF
251	CLS
252	UNPLOT
253	CLEAR
254	RETURN
255	COPY

Programs

This section of the book contains a number of programs: games as well as more serious applications. Games are not only entertaining, but can also be very instructive, and it can be very interesting to find out how things are expressed in BASIC. A number of the programs are designed to carry out statistical calculations. Before you look at the programs themselves, here are a few points to remember.

All these programs have been tested. The line numbers often go up in 2s to save memory space. With some programs even a small alteration can be fatal.

All the programs can be used with the standard 1K memory.

Be especially careful when typing in the symbols **, < >, < = and > =. These symbols must always be entered in a single keystroke.

On the ZX80 computer, PAUSE instructions are always followed by POKE 16437,255.

In most cases you can check whether you have entered the program correctly by comparing it with the example. If results are obtained by means of RND functions there may be differences.

The empty string "" is typed by pressing " twice and not by pressing the Q key.

The program CENTURY CALENDAR is based on an idea

found in a manual for HP calculators (HP-45 applications book), and the program MOON LANDER is based on an idea described in a manual for Texas Instruments SR52. The other programs are either based on the usual standard formulas or are, as far as we know, original.

In the example programs, items to be entered by the user are underlined.

This is an amusing program that will help young children to develop their mathematical skills. You can choose from addition, subtraction, and multiplication by typing in +, – or *. The computer will then show you ten simple sums. Each number consists of only one digit. If a wrong answer is given twice to the same problem, the computer will automatically show the correct answer. The score at the end of the program consists of the number of mistakes made, so the ideal score is 0.

Program

```
 2  PRINT "CHOOSE +,–, OR*"
 4  INPUT K$
 6  LET X=Ø
 8  FOR K=1 TO 1Ø
1Ø  PAUSE 75
12  POKE 16437,255          (Only for ZX80)
14  CLS
16  LET F=0
18  PRINT "SUM ";K
2Ø  LET A=INT(RND*9+1.)
22  LET B=INT(RND*9+1.)
```

```
24  IF B > A THEN GOSUB 6Ø
26  LET CK=CODE K$
28  IF CK=21 THEN LET C=A+B
3Ø  IF CK=22 THEN LET C=A–B
32  IF CK=23 THEN LET C=A*B
34  PRINT A;CHR$ CK;B;"="
36  PRINT "INPUT NUMBER"
38  INPUT AN
4Ø  LET F=F+1
42  IF C–AN=0 THEN LET G$="CORRECT"
44  IF C–AN < >Ø THEN LET G$= "WRONG"
46  IF C–AN < >Ø THEN LET X=X+1
48  PRINT AN;" IS ";G$
5Ø  IF F=2 THEN PRINT "ANSWER=";C
52  IF F=2 THEN GOTO 56
54  IF C–AN < >Ø THEN GOTO 36
56  NEXT K
58  PRINT "SCORE=";X
6Ø  LET H=A
62  LET A=B
64  LET B=H
66  RETURN
```

Example

```
CHOOSE+, –, OR*
±
SUM 1
7 + 3 =
INPUT NUMBER
1Ø
1Ø IS CORRECT
SUM 2
7 + 5 =
INPUT NUMBER, etc.
```

MASTERMIND

One of the most popular games of the last few years is the game of MASTERMIND. Its main charm is no doubt its simplicity. The original game is played with colored pegs. The computer uses digits. The computer has hidden 4 digits in 4 compartments and you must try to guess these digits by naming 4 numbers each time. The computer then reports how many figures out of the 4 quoted by you are actually in the hidden compartments and also how many of them are in the correct sequence. For example, if the computer has chosen the sequence 1 5 4 7 and you name 4 5 3 8, the computer reports "2 NUMBERS CORRECT" (4 and 5) and "1 IN CORRECT PLACE" (5).

If you do not yet possess the original game, you will no doubt hurry to the shop after trying it out with the program given below. To make it a little easier for you, the computer always chooses 4 different digits.

Program

```
 5  DIM A(4)
 7  DIM B(4)
 9  RAND O
11  LET N=Ø
13  FOR K=1 TO 4
15  LET A(K)=INT(RND*9+1.)
17  NEXT K
19  FOR K=1 TO 3
21  FOR J=K+1 TO 4
23  IF A(K)=A(J) THEN GOTO 13
25  NEXT J
27  NEXT K
29  FOR K=1 TO 4
31  PRINT "NUMBER";K;"="
33  INPUT B(K)
35  PRINT B(K)
37  NEXT K
39  LET N=N+1
41  LET G=Ø
43  LET P=Ø
45  FOR K=1 TO 4
```

```
47  FOR J=1 TO 4
49  IF A(K)=B(J) THEN LET G=G+1
51  NEXT J
53  IF A(K)=B(K) THEN LET P=P+1
55  NEXT K
57  PRINT G;" NUMBERS CORRECT"
59  PRINT P;" IN CORRECT PLACE"
61  PAUSE 15Ø
63  POKE 16437,255        (Only for ZX80)
65  CLS
67  IF P= 4 THEN GOTO 71
69  GOTO 29
71  PRINT "OK SCORE=";N
```

Example

```
NUMBER 1 =
3
NUMBER 2 =
5
NUMBER 3 =
1
NUMBER 4 =
7
2 NUMBERS CORRECT
Ø IN CORRECT PLACE
NUMBER 1 =
etc.
```

SAVING 1

The following program shows the amount that is saved if you deposit a certain amount each term. The final amount naturally depends on the interest rate and the number of times you have deposited the chosen amount.

Program

```
 10 PRINT "SAVING"
 20 PRINT "INTEREST="
 30 INPUT J
 40 PRINT J
 50 LET J=J*0.01
 60 PRINT "AMOUNT PER TERM="
 70 INPUT PMT
 80 PRINT PMT
 90 PRINT "NUMBER OF TERMS="
100 INPUT N
110 PRINT N
120 LET TEL= ((J+1)**N-1)*PMT
130 PRINT "FUTURE VALUE=";TEL/J
```

Example

SAVING

```
INTEREST =
8
AMOUNT PER TERM =
1ØØØ
NUMBER OF TERMS =
5
FUTURE VALUE = 5866.6Ø1
```

This example shows that if you pay $1000 into your savings, account for 5 years running (interest 8%), you will in the end have saved $5866.60.

In line 20 you see the symbol **; this is to be typed in by pressing the H key.

MORE SAVING

This program is a continuation of *Saving*. Now ask how a specified total amount can be reached if you know the interest rate and the number of terms.

Program

```
 10 PRINT "PAYMENT PER TERM"
 20 PRINT "INTEREST="
 30 INPUT J
 40 PRINT J
 50 PRINT "FUTURE VALUE="
 60 INPUT FV
 70 PRINT FV
 80 PRINT "NUMBER OF TERMS="
 90 INPUT N
100 PRINT N
110 LET DEN=FV*J*0.01
120 LET NUM=(1+0.01*J)**N-1
130 LET PMT = DEN/NUM
140 PRINT "TO BE PAID PER TERM=";PMT
```

Example

```
PAYMENT PER TERM
INTEREST =
8
FUTURE VALUE =
10000
NUMBER OF TERMS =
5
TO BE PAID PER TERM = 1704.56
```

MEAN AND STANDARD DEVIATION

Mean and standard deviation are two pillars in statistics. The mean is found by taking the sum of the numbers and dividing this value by the number of numbers (N). The standard deviation is based on the difference between each value and the mean. All these differences are squared and then added up. This value is then divided by N–1 and the square root of the result ultimately gives us the standard deviation. The above sentences are in fact expressed much more briefly by the program. The program first asks for the number of values after which each value is entered separately.

Program

```
 10 PRINT "NUMBER OF VALUES="
 20 INPUT N
 30 LET S=0
 40 LET S2=0
 50 FORK=1 TO N
 60 PRINT "INPUT NUMBER ";K;"
 70 INPUT X
 80 CLS
 90 LET S=S+X
100 LET S2=S2+X*X
110 NEXT K
120 PRINT "MEAN=";S/N
130 LET V=(S2-S*S/N)/(N-1)
140 PRINT "S.DEV=";SQR(V)
```

Example

```
NUMBER OF VALUES=
4
INPUT NUMBER 1
4
INPUT NUMBER 2
4
INPUT NUMBER 3
5
INPUT NUMBER 4
4
MEAN =4.25
S.DEV=0.5
```

REGRESSION AND CORRELATION

Regression and correlation calculus is used to find the best way of drawing a straight line connecting a given number of points. This straight line is defined by two magnitudes, the angle of inclination (M) and the point where the line crosses the Y axis (B). Each point is defined by an X coordinate and a Y coordinate. The program asks first of all how many points there are. When the coordinates have been input the values, M and B are calculated. Finally the correlation coefficient R is displayed. If all points are in a straight line the absolute value of R will be 1. If the points are not exactly in a straight line, the absolute value of R will be less than 1. Evidently, this value of R indicates how close the points are to the calculated straight line.

Program

```
  5  PRINT "N="
 1Ø  INPUT N
 15  PRINT N
 2Ø  LET XS=Ø
 25  LET YS=Ø
 3Ø  LET X2=Ø
 35  LET Y2=Ø
 4Ø  LET XY=0
 45  FOR K=1 TO N
 5Ø  PRINT "X";K;"="
 55  INPUT X
 6Ø  PRINT X
 65  PRINT "Y";K;"="
 7Ø  INPUT Y
 75  PRINT Y
 8Ø  PAUSE 75
 85  POKE 16437,255          (Only for ZX80)
 9Ø  CLS
 95  LET XS=XS+X
1ØØ  LET YS=YS+Y
1Ø5  LET X2=X2+X*X
11Ø  LET Y2=Y2+Y*Y
115  LET XY=XY+X*Y
```

```
120 NEXT K
125 LET M=(XS*YS/N-XY)/(XS*XS/N-X2)
130 PRINT "M=";M
135 PRINT "B=";YS/N-M*XS/N
140 LET NM=SQR((N*X2-XS*XS)*(N*Y2-YS*YS))
145 LET T=N*XY-XS*YS
150 PRINT "R=";T/NM
```

Example

```
N=
2
2
X1=
1
Y1=
2
X2=
2
Y2=
4
M=2
B=0
R=1
```

FACTORIAL

The factorial of a number is the value obtained by carrying out the following operation: number * (number – 1) * (number – 2) ... * 2 * 1 =. For instance, the factorial of 3 is 3*2*1 = 6.

The factorial of 3 is written 3! The factorial indicates in how many ways we can arrange a number of objects. Thus 3 objects can be arranged in 6 different ways. The program starts from whole (positive) numbers.

Program

```
10 PRINT "INPUT N"
20 INPUT N
30 LET F=N
40 IF N=1 OR N=0 THEN LET F=1
50 IF N=1 OR N=0 THEN GOTO 90
60 LET F=F*(N-1)
70 LET N=N-1
80 IF N > 1 THEN GOTO 60
90 PRINT "FACTORIAL=";F
```

Example

```
INPUT N
3
FACTORIAL = 6
```

COMBINATIONS

Suppose that you have n different objects (n is 7, for example). You can then ask in how many ways you can arrange these into rows of m objects (m is 5, for example). This number is written $\genfrac{}{}{0pt}{}{n}{m}$ and pronounced "n over m." It is equal to the factorial of n, divided by the factorial of m times the factorial of n-m. These values are sometimes referred to as binomial coefficients. See also Permutations that follows.

Program

```
 1Ø  PRINT "N="
 2Ø  INPUT N
 3Ø  PRINT "M="
 4Ø  INPUT M
 5Ø  LET F=N
 6Ø  GOSUB 3ØØ
 7Ø  LET NA=FA
 8Ø  LET F=M
 9Ø  GOSUB 3ØØ
1ØØ  LET T1=FA
11Ø  LET F=N-M
12Ø  GOSUB 3ØØ
13Ø  LET T2=FA
```

```
140  PRINT "C=";NA/(T1*T2)
150  STOP
300  IF F=0 OR F=1 THEN LET FA=1
310  IF F=0 OR F=1 THEN GOTO 360
320  LET FA=F
330  LET FA=FA*(F-1)
340  LET F=F-1
350  IF F < 1 THEN GOTO 330
360  RETURN
```

Example

```
N=
7
M=
5
C=21
```

PERMUTATIONS

Suppose you have a number of objects, 8, for example. How many ways you can arrange them in rows of m objects (m may be 4, for example) taking into account the sequence in which they are arranged (thus the series a b c d is different from the series a c b d as the sequence is different).

The following example will serve as an illustration. Suppose you have 13 playing cards (2 of hearts to ace of hearts). If you ask, how many different combinations of 7 cards can be found?, this is a combination as the sequence is not important. If you ask, "How many possibilities are there, including sequences?", you are dealing with permutations.

The number of permutations is calculated by dividing the factorial of n by the factorial of n-m.

Program

```
 1Ø  PRINT "N="
 2Ø  INPUT N
 3Ø  PRINT "M="
 4Ø  INPUT M
 5Ø  LET F=N
 6Ø  GOSUB 300
 7Ø  LET NA=FA
 8Ø  LET F=N–M
 9Ø  GOSUB 300
1ØØ  LET T=FA
11Ø  PRINT "P=";NA/T
12Ø  STOP
3ØØ  IF F=Ø OR F=1 THEN LET FA=1
31Ø  IF F=Ø OR F=1 THEN GOTO 36Ø
32Ø  LET FA=F
33Ø  LET FA=FA*(F–1)
34Ø  LET F=F–1
35Ø  IF F > 1 THEN GOTO 33Ø
36Ø  RETURN
```

Example

N=

8

```
M=
4
P=1680
```

If you frequently need to calculate both combinations and permutations, the program Combinations can be expanded simply by adding the line:

```
145  PRINT "P=";NA/T2
```

NORMAL DISTRIBUTION

In statistics, normal or Gaussian distribution plays a very important part. The following program calculates for a random variable X the chance that a value is found which is less than X, if the results are distributed normally. The normal distribution has a theoretical mean 0 and a standard variance 1. In line 50 you will see the expression PI. This corresponds to the π symbol under the M key.

Program

```
 10 PRINT "X="
 20 INPUT X
 30 PRINT X
 40 LET T=1/(1+0.2316419*X)
 50 LET C=1/SQR(2*PI)
 60 LET FD=EXP(-X*X/2)*C
 70 LET A1=0.3193815*T
 80 LET A2=-0.356563782*T*T
 90 LET A3=1.781477937*T*T*T
100 LET A4=-1.821255978*T*T*T*T
110 LET A5=1.330274429*T*T*T*T*T
120 LET F=1-FD*(A1+A2+A3+A4+A5)
130 PRINT "F=";F
```

Example

```
X=
1.645
F=0.95001511
```

POISSON DISTRIBUTION

The poisson distribution is coupled to the so-called statistic of rare events. Chances related to such things as lightning strikes, road accidents, and so on are usually coupled to this distribution. Only two values are asked for: L, which represents the mean value, and K, which represents the number of times for which the chance is calculated.

The following example will illustrate this. Suppose that in the last 50 years there have been 85 lightning strikes in a certain area, and in a certain month, May for example. This gives an average L of 85/50 = 1.7 lightning strikes for the month of May. With the aid of this program, you can then calculate the chance that there will be exactly 6 lightning strikes in the next month of May. The example following the program shows that this chance P =0.006 . . . .

Remember that the symbol ** in line 60 must always be entered in a single keystroke (shifted H).

Program

```
 10Ø  PRINT "L="
 20Ø  INPUT L
 30Ø  PRINT "K="
 40Ø  INPUT K
 50Ø  LET T1=EXP(-L)
 60Ø  LET T2=L**K
 70Ø  LET F=K
 80Ø  GOSUB 300Ø
 90Ø  LET N=FA
100Ø  LET P= T1*T2/N
110Ø  PRINT "L=";L
120Ø  PRINT "K=";K
130Ø  PRINT "P=";P
140Ø  STOP
300Ø  IF F=Ø OR F=1 THEN LET FA=1
310Ø  IF F=Ø OR F=1 THEN GOTO 360Ø
320Ø  LET FA=F
330Ø  LET FA=FA*(F-1)
340Ø  LET F=F-1
350Ø  IF F > 1 THEN GOTO 330Ø
360Ø  RETURN
```

Example

L
1.7
K
6
L=1.7
K=6
P=.ØØ61243558

FIBONACCI

The Fibonacci series is produced by starting with 1 and adding the last two numbers to arrive at the next. This series has a number of remarkable properties. The ratio between any two adjacent Fibonacci numbers after 3 is about 1 : 1.6. This is the so-called Golden Ratio.

Program

```
 10 PRINT "FIBONACCI SERIES"
 20 LET T1=1
 30 LET T2=1
 40 PRINT "INPUT NUMBER OF TERMS"
 50 INPUT N
 60 PRINT "T1=";T1
 70 PRINT "T2=";T2
 80 FOR K=3 TO N
 90 LET TB=T2
100 LET T2=T2+T1
110 LET T1=TB
120 PRINT "T";K;"=";T2
130 NEXT K
```

Example

```
FIBONACCI SERIES
INPUT NUMBER
7
T1=1
T2=1
T3=2
T4=3
T5=5
T6=8
T7=13
```

INTEGRATION

The following program calculates the integral of a function F(X) between the boundaries A and B.

First, the program asks for the number of steps in which the integral will be calculated. The program uses Simpson's rule. The function is placed in a subroutine: lines 300 to 320. The function in our example program is the function X^3, X*X*X.

Program

```
 1Ø  PRINT "NUMBER OF STEPS"
 2Ø  INPUT N
 25  PRINT N
 3Ø  PRINT "A="
 4Ø  INPUT A
 45  PRINT A
 5Ø  PRINT "B="
 6Ø  INPUT B
 65  PRINT B
 7Ø  LET S=(B-A)/N
 75  LET SUM=Ø
 8Ø  FOR K=1 TO N-1
 9Ø  LET E=INT(K/2)-K/2
1ØØ  LET X=A+K*S
11Ø  LET C=4
12Ø  IF E=Ø THEN LET C=2
13Ø  GOSUB 3ØØ
14Ø  LET SUM=SUM+C*F
15Ø  NEXT K
16Ø  LET X=A
17Ø  GOSUB 3ØØ
18Ø  LET FA=F
19Ø  LET X=B
2ØØ  GOSUB 3ØØ
21Ø  LET FB=F
22Ø  LET J=S/3*(FA+SUM+FB)
23Ø  PRINT "INT=";J
24Ø  STOP
3ØØ  REM FUNCTION
```

```
310 LET F=X*X*X
320 RETURN
```

Example

```
NUMBER OF STEPS
20
A=
0
B=
2
INT=4
```

In this example the integral of the function $F(X) = X^3$ was calculated, between the boundaries 0 and 2. If you want to calculate, for example, the integral of the function $2X^2 + 3X$ (between the boundaries A and B), you only need to replace line 310 by:

```
310 LET F = 2*X*X+3*X
```

THROWING RINGS

You are throwing a ring at a target that is 9 meters away. The target is 1 meter high. Each time you throw you can state the speed and angle of the throw. There are of course only three possibilities: the ring does not reach the target, the ring passes over the target, and the ring hits the target. The angle must always be given in degrees. Even a programmer with an unsteady hand will be able to hit the target without fail after some practice!

Remember that PI is entered by pressing the M key (π).

Program

```
 10  PRINT "INPUT SPEED"
 20  INPUT V
 30  PRINT "INPUT ANGLE"
 40  INPUT A
 50  CLS
 60  LET A=A*2*PI/360
 70  LET SA=SIN(A)
 80  LET CA=COS(A)
 90  LET T=V*SA/5+.2
100  LET S=V*CA*T
```

```
110  IF S > 10 THEN PRINT "TOO FAR"
120  IF S < 9 THEN PRINT "NOT FAR ENOUGH"
130  IF ABS(S-9.5) > =0.5 THEN GOTO 10
140  PRINT "HIT"
```

Example

```
INPUT SPEED
6
INPUT ANGLE
30
NOT FAR ENOUGH
INPUT SPEED
13
INPUT ANGLE
45
TOO FAR
INPUT SPEED
etc.
```

MOON LANDER

You are in a moon lander 200 meters above the surface of the Moon and your speed of descent is −20m/s. You can reduce this speed by firing the retrorocket. This will of course use up fuel (for even on the moon you don't get something for nothing). Each time you fire the retrorocket, you can state how much fuel is used. At the start there are 100 liters left in the tank. Each time the computer gives you the amount of fuel, the speed of descent (v), and the height (DIST).

Program

```
 1Ø  LET V=-2Ø
 2Ø  LET S=2ØØ
 3Ø  LET TA=1ØØ
 4Ø  PRINT "INPUT FUEL"
 5Ø  INPUT FUEL
 6Ø  CLS
 7Ø  LET TA=TA-FUEL
 8Ø  LET A= FUEL -1
 9Ø  LET V=V+A
1ØØ  LET S=S+V-A/2
11Ø  PRINT "FUEL=";TA
```

```
120 PRINT "V=";V
130 PRINT "DIST=";S
140 IF ABS(V) < .5 AND ABS(S) < .5 THEN GOTO 200
150 IF V > 0 THEN PRINT "GOING UP"
160 IF TA < = 0 THEN PRINT "TANK EMPTY"
170 IF TA > 0 and S > 0 THEN GOTO 40
180 PRINT "FAILED"
190 STOP
200 PRINT "LANDED"
```

Example

```
INPUT FUEL
5
FUEL = 95
V=- 16
DIST=182
INPUT FUEL
5
FUEL=90
V=-12
DIST=168
INPUT FUEL
etc.
```

TARGET

Target is a very simple game. The computer asks you each time to state an X coordinate and a Y coordinate and thus to find an invisible target. You can enter any of the numbers 1 to 20. The program records how many turns you need to reach your goal. Each time you have entered an X coordinate and a Y coordinate, the computer provides useful information such as whether we need to move to the right or to the left and whether you need to go up or down.

Program

```
 10 RAND 0
 20 LET P=INT(RND*20+1.0)
 30 LET Q=INT(RND*20+1.0)
 40 LET Z=1
 50 PRINT "INPUT X"
 60 INPUT X
 70 PRINT "INPUT Y"
 80 INPUT Y
 90 LET Z=Z+1
100 CLS
110 IF P-X > 0 THEN PRINT "RIGHT"
120 IF X-P > 0 THEN PRINT "LEFT"
130 IF Q-Y > 0 THEN PRINT "UP"
140 IF Y-Q > 0 THEN PRINT "DOWN"
150 LET A=(P-X)*(P-X)+(Q-Y)*(Q-Y)
160 IF A > 0.1 THEN GOTO 50
170 PRINT "SUCCEEDED IN";Z;"TURNS"
```

Example

```
INPUT X
5
INPUT Y
10
RIGHT
UP
INPUT X
etc.
```

CENTURY CALENDAR

This program finds out on which day of the week each date of this century and the last century fell or will fall. All items need to be input as numbers. The example program finds the day on which 30 August 1981 fell.

Program

```
 1Ø  PRINT "DAY="
 2Ø  INPUT D
 3Ø  PRINT D
 4Ø  PRINT "MONTH="
 5Ø  INPUT M
 6Ø  PRINT M
 7Ø  PRINT "YEAR="
 8Ø  INPUT Y
 9Ø  PRINT Y
1ØØ  IF M< =2 THEN LET Y=Y-1
11Ø  IF M< =2 THEN LET M=M+12
12Ø  LET E=INT((13/5)*(M+1))
13Ø  LET F=INT(5*Y/4)
14Ø  LET G=INT(Y/400)
```

```
150 LET H=INT(Y/400)
160 LET T=D+E+F-G+H
170 LET DA=INT((T/7-INT(T/7))*7+0.1)
180 PRINT "SA=0, SU=1, MO=2"
190 PRINT "TU=3, WE=4, THU=5"
200 PRINT "FR=6"
210 PRINT "DAY=";DA
```

Example

```
DAY
30
MONTH
8
YEAR
1981
SA=0, SU=1, MO=2
TU=3, WE=4, THU=5
FR=6
DAY=1
```

GUESSING ANIMAL NAMES

This game shows the possibilities offered by the ZX81 when it comes to manipulating letters. Each time you give the RUN command the name of an animal appears on the screen, but the letters are not in the familiar order. All the animal names are in fact hidden in the string variable P$. For clarity it has been divided into a number of sections in our program. You need to type in the letters immediately following one another, so they must not be separated by any spaces.

Program

```
 5  RAND
 7  DIM A$(10,5)
 9  DIM B$ (5,1)
11  LET G$=""
13  LET P$="EKANSREGITTUORT
            REDDAESROHELAHW
            ESUOMLIANSPEEHS
            KROTS"
15  FOR K=1 TO 10
17  LET B1=(K-1)*5+1
19  LET A$ (K)=P$(B1+4)
21  NEXT K
```

```
23  LET R=INT(RND*1Ø+1.)
25  FOR K=5 TO 1 STEP -1
27  LET B$(K)=A$(R,K)
29  LET G$=G$+B$(K)
31  NEXT K
33  LET X$=""
35  LET R=INT(RND*5+1.)
37  FOR K=R TO R+4
39  LET L=K
41  IF K>5 THEN LET L=L-5
43  LET X$=X$+B$(L)
45  NEXT K
47  PRINT X$
49  PRINT "IS A=?"
51  INPUT M$
53  CLS
55  IF M$ < > G$ THEN PRINT "WRONG"
57  IF M$ < > G$ THEN GOTO 47
59  PRINT "CORRECT"
```

Example

ITREG
IS A=?
<u>TREIG</u>
WRONG
ITREG
IS A=?
<u>TIGER</u>
CORRECT

Index

Index

Notes

Notes

Notes

Notes

Notes

Notes

Notes

Notes